THE NORDIC
TABLE

HELLE STANGERUP

THE NORDIC TABLE

– over time

HØST & SØN

THE NORDIC TABLE
First published in 2001 by Høst & Søn as
Tidens Bord

© *Helle Stangerup* and Høst & Søn 2002
© Illustrations, see page 181

Translated by Erik Tillisch and Tony Wedgwood
Illustration editor: *Helle Stangerup*
Graphic designed and typesetting: *Freddy Pedersen*
Printed in Danmark by Abildgaard Grafisk
Binding by Chr. Hendriksen og søn A/S, Skive

Printet in Denmark 2002

ISBN 87-14-24982-0

HØST & SØN · KØBMAGERGADE 62 · 1150 KØBENHAVN K
www.hoest.dk

Table of contents

Foreword

"The Nordic table – over time" is a series of essays spanning from the year 1500 to our time. It is divided into seven sections, each with its own theme. The first, second and fourth sections are set in one particular period, representing the eras of the Renaissance, the Absolute Monarchy and Victorianism until the First World War respectively. The third part crosses all time periods but is restricted to its subject: Nordic porcelain and Flora Danica. The same is true of the fifth and sixth sections, which deal with faience and outdoor life. The final passage brings us up to our time.

This book would not have been completed had it not been for the unique support offered by art historians and other scholars. To museums, libraries, auction houses, private companies and Royal Scandinavia: I am greatly indebted to every one of them.

The bed and the table are man's most fundamental pieces of furniture. As life is normally conceived in the former, it is either prolonged or shortened at the latter. Thus "The Nordic table – over time".

Helle Stangerup
April 2002

From Bread

to White Gold

The Table

The table stands close to the hearth. It is laid with slices of bread to use as plates. Salt cellars are evenly distributed along its planks and in the centre steam rises from a large bowl filled with fat meat stew.

Cutlery is limited solely to the diners´ own weapon – a knife. The beer is ready to be poured into horn or mug to be passed around. It is an ordinary day, close to 5 p.m and heads are bowed while grace is said. Now the meal can begin.

This scene is set in Denmark around the year 1500. In the summer one got up with the sun at 3 a.m.; in the winter the church bells chimed a couple of hours later to get people out of their beds or alcoves.

Real manor houses were yet to come, and royal castles were fortresses, built for combat not comfort. Of course, the wealthy could afford better food and items with which to decorate their homes, but when faced with the vagaries of nature, all were equally vulnerable to the same powerful forces of darkness and cold.

Windows were nailed shut and had panes fashioned from horn or oiled paper. Each home produced its own few tallow candles, while only princes and the Church could afford to use candles made from bee's wax.

So life indoors was spent in the gloom, with the flames from the hearth as the main source of light. And as for warmth, the hearth rewarded the providers of its greedy use of firewood by ungratefully sending most of its heat straight up the chimney.

Fur coats and leather stockings were worn indoors from early autumn until spring. And when the frost tightened its grip, the contributions from all available bodily warmth was needed from master, servant and beasts alike, which explained the stench of rot, dirt, sweat and damp pelts.

Change was bound to come from the south. When the Renaissance finally arrived, one invention was to provide an invaluable entrée to the harsh north. The flighty, faithless flames could be tamed and controlled in the closed stove.

These smoky, sooty monstrosities, consisting of nothing more than earthen pots stuck together, were soon refined and made more efficient. And the standard of clothing, architecture – indeed the entire pattern of social life - began to change as the stoves made possible a lifestyle that until now had only been possible in milder climates.

On the heels of the burst of creativity, culture and thirst for knowledge brought about by the Renaissance, appreciation of everyday aesthetics followed. It was to transform the two most important items of furniture, that great duo of pleasure – the bed and the table.

A depiction of the most celebrated of meals, The Last Supper. Knives are visible alongside large bowls of food, salt and beverages.
The puffy objects are called hard tack, a type of roll baked with wheaten flour, while the pointed loaves are made of thin strudel pastry.
In the centre of the table is a wine chalice. Its shape was to become the standard for the common drinking glass. The tablecloth is presumably made of fustian.

Table Linen

The tablecloth was a familiar sight. It covered the alter in front of everybody´s eyes sunday upon sunday.

Going to church not only eased the soul's path to salvation, it also appealed to a fundamental yearning for beauty in a harsh way of life. Choirs, frescoes, carvings adorning the altarpiece, and, during Catholicism, also the images of saints and the smell of incense, they were all unattainable belongings of The Divine.

But the cloth was different. It could be copied and in the secular world it thrived, folded, tucked under, sometimes even in three layers. The bottom layer was dark and in better households it was often made of velvet or gold embroidered silk or even tapestry.

About the year 1500 Flemish textile manufacturers masterminded a technique by which linen could feature spectacular damask weaving. This product was immediately accepted by the wealthy at the expense of fustian and drill. However it did not solve the problem of the state of fingers after their deep dive into the greasy food.

Naturally hands were washed. The priest did so before and after communion, and that ritual had since long ago influenced the homes of both rich and poor.

One sat down at the table and left it again with clean hands – that was as certain as saying Grace. But during the meal the remains of the fatty meat was wiped off the fingers on the tablecloth.

The stage was set for the discovery of the napkin. The French called it "doublier", a sort of extra cloth that was either fixed to the table or was passed around the diners. Eventually it was cut up and handed individually to each participant in the meal.

Detail from a tablecloth in blue and white, woven in Copenhagen 1621.

The Italian sense of refinement seemed limitless. With deft fingers the napkin could be folded into the shape of a flower or a fan, or it might contain small gifts or even surprises such as little birds, which would flutter up from their confinement and fly out the open windows.

No such examples of creativity are known from the Nordic countries.

Certainly the nailed-up windows would prevent the escape of any small birds.

However, for a short time, Denmark boasted her own silk weaving mill, and its quality and motifs easily matched European standards. Here the symbols of royal power were displayed: the king's initials, his proud fleet on the oceans, and, as we are to see later, even table decorations and highlights from the menu.

*Even in a close family circle the division of sexes by the table
was observed. Here we see Jacob Ulfeldt and Birgitte Brockenhuus with
ten sons, six daughters and the dog. Glass ornaments at the table
appear to be Italian, as does the setting.*

Seating and Serving

For the most part the seats were solid benches. Just three sides of the table were occupied, while the facing edge was left open so as to facilitate serving. This pattern was maintained while seating of diners changed during the 16th century.

Royal ordinances of those days dealt with even minute details of daily life including, of course, morality. To prevent common good humour from escalating into anything intimate, it was resolved that men and women be seperated during meals.

During the Catholic period what might occur in bed was hardly of any serious concern. After all Letters of Indulgence took care of all kinds of sins.

Luther´s Reformation, however, tightened the grip on morals. At that time, too, syphilis struck and this was a case of earthly punishment for earthly sins – absolution or not.

Eventually society gave in to the king's command. Women would sit to the left, men to the right. Besides, just that pattern had emerged in the churches as pews were manoeuvred into place, so the subject touched upon the most important of all: The Hereafter.

Not that this put an end to all merriment. Presently new decrees followed, such as when musicians were ordered not to strike up until after everybody had risen. Otherwise girls, eager to dance, jumped over the table and on to the floor, much to the horror and discomfort of the elderly and weak.

Serving was a man's job. Among peasants, of course, waiters performed only at major events and were then recruited among available farm workers. These were strictly instructed not to look hungrily into the food but instead fix a respectful look at their master.

Better-off households would draw upon younger relatives or local schoolboys for a few pennies, and at court it was considered an honour for quite young sons of the nobility to carry the king's dishes.

Princes of those days suffered a constant fear of getting poisoned. As a result the cupbearer enjoyed respect, so much the more as he took upon him the plight of a potential victim by personally swallowing the first sip.

In southern countries serving included an additional array of qualifications such as "delicate, noble, subtle white hands". In the North, however, a cupbearer would be accepted if only adequately fed, well washed and with no warts on his fingers.

Mastering the knife when attacking the roast was a far more demanding task. The carver must tackle entire carcasses of oxen, swine or stags besides all kinds of birds such as swans, cranes or exotic pea-cocks. Not only did it require elaborate craftsmanship, but also a thorough know-ledge of anatomy.

Top performers might show off by carv-ing items in mid air, all according to such sophisticated rituals as to inspire literary works on the subject.

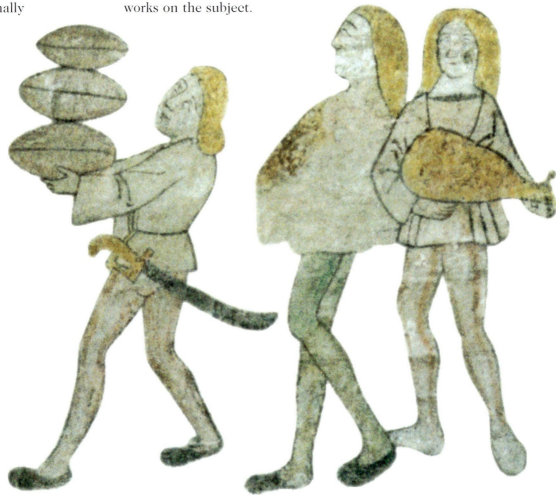

Young menservants carry in the dishes. A full ham and three dishes, one on top of the other.

Cutlery

Spoon and knife were personal belongings. The spoon sprang from the age-old ladle, which at some time was furnished with a handle. While the handle was short, the width of the spoon afforded a sound mouthful, as also it allowed space for religious or personal inscriptions.

The knife entered this world as a weapon, as seen by its sharp point. It was also useful for extracting lumps of meat from the common bowl, but less practical for buttering the bread, so here the thumb came in handy.

A third contender, however, attempted to gatecrash into the established company: the fork.

A Byzantine princess who disliked touching the food used a little fork with two prongs. It happened as early as in the 11th century but left only slight traces.

Of course there was the large frying fork

besides some evidence of tiny fruit forks, but not until the late 15th century did the fork appear openly and confidently. It happened in the city-state of Venice, where it enjoyed general acceptance – until trouble started.

This eating utensil, it was found, bore alarming resemblance to the trident held by Lucifer himself, so the clergy rose against it in defence of Christianity. Surely the good Lord had equipped Man with five fingers to enable him to eat with them, not to see him handling the Devil´s tool instead. As far north as in Germany clergy thundered against such an abomination brought about by Satan himself. The campaign ultimately managed to drive the hygienic little tool back into oblivion.

One hundred years later the fork emerged again at the French court of Henry III.

This court was already the epicentre of the weird and twisted, advanced sex and novel stimuli such as snuff; since the fork invited to affected mannerism it was given both recognition and shelter.

This, however, was true only for the set-up of "les Mignons", those royal favourites. The outside world scoffed at this new implement and dumped it into the abyss of ridicule.

Man's manners at the dining table have been subject to intense scrutiny at all times. Here the mythical dividing line between "them" and "us" is drawn, and even the slightest deviation may set the subtle balance in jeopardy. An upstart such as the fork was helplessly bound to have shortcomings in this delicate power-game between the slightly rude side and that of the affected.

In Shakespeare's England it was not until 1611 that the traveller and author Thomas Coryat first mentioned the small instrument which he encountered on a journey to Italy. But he was given little praise for bringing one home as a souvenir.

Neither would Louis XIV here of any such tomfoolery at his table. Nor did he need it. Saint-Simon described the elegance with which the Sun King ate even stew with his fingers and yet left his garb perfectly spotless.

At the same time, however, sets of cutlery including the fork were fashioned for decorative purposes, often to be given as

A spoon in your hat, is a spoon in your hand.

The Woman to the left holds a fork on which the two prongs have expanded to three. The infant to the right appears to leak a bit.

THE NORDIC TABLE

Part of the same tablecloth as shown on page 12. Scattered over the table forks clearly appear together with knives and a light sprinkle of flowers. Other motifs include a pea fowl, lobster, sturgeon and fruits such as grapes. The turkey appears somewhat flattened.

princely gifts, and the splendour knew no end with their handles fashioned from coral, mother of pearl or semiprecious stones.

Certainly the first known Danish fork belonged to king Christian IV. It is shown on p. 17 in a set fashioned from enamelled gold and agate and so delicate that it was hardly meant to be used.

Not until the 18 th century was the fork given unconditional respectability as a full member of the cutlery family and then only on the most distinguished tables.

During the long wait improvements had been made, which added to its stature: the two prongs had grown to three or four.

The spoon on the other hand had slimmed and adapted a narrower shape, while the knife was moderated – now it could be used for no other purposes than eating.

Indeed it was a less than pleasing sight to watch knives being used for tooth picking, and besides there were all sensible reasons to ban pointed weapons from about the table. Consequently the blade was rounded off.

But in the humble homes, those in which the two ancient implements were roosting in hats or belts or on the rafter overhead, the fork was not easily accepted

It took several generations before it reached in the hands of common people.

Salt, Finery – and Horror

In the days of the Renaissance consumption of the vital element salt far exceeded that of the present time. To this was added its function as the most important means of preserving food.

For this reason salt inspired profound religious awe as reflected in certain languages. In Hebrew, for instance, salted food simply meant sacred food and it was handled with corresponding veneration.

Certainly saltcellars were of appreciable size, but one could not simply scoop into them. Three fingers would suffice, and spilling salt invited misfortune, not to mention upsetting a whole cellar, which could have the gravest of consequences.

The ship symbolised the Church itself. To a Christian prince there was nothing like keeping his own personal salt in "la nef", a table ship typically fashioned from precious metal and elaborately adorned. Moreover the ship would protect its contents from poison, and in this capacity it was also put to use for items like cutlery and napkins.

One amusing specimen belonged to Johan III of Sweden. This treasure could be wound and make a tour of the table much to the delight of the king and his guests.

One of the silver-gilded ships,
that adorned distinguished tables
in the 16th century.

Festivities called for adornment, for adornments result in pleasure. Nature's creations were put to use such as flowers and leaves. In time, however, more refinement would be wanted.

The showdish entered Denmark by way of Germany. It consisted of an odd mixture of the edible and the decorative; in the beginning just as a modelled stag with a cover of sweet frosting or as roast poultry with its plumage slipped back on.

The craze escalated. Pies and marzipan were coated with gilt, and the cathedral of Cologne rose in all its splendour. Frameworks had to be constructed to support such clever panoramas as complete mountain works, Greek temples and Diana hunting across Roman hills.

Just like all whims get out of hand the show dish lost fashion's good graces and was brought to an end in most countries. In Denmark it was terminated by yet another decree, this one in 1643.

When Hieronymus Bosch went exploring in the depths of horror all bounds were burst. Apparently his guests were unaware of the ancient English proverb: "It takes a long spoon to dine with the Devil".

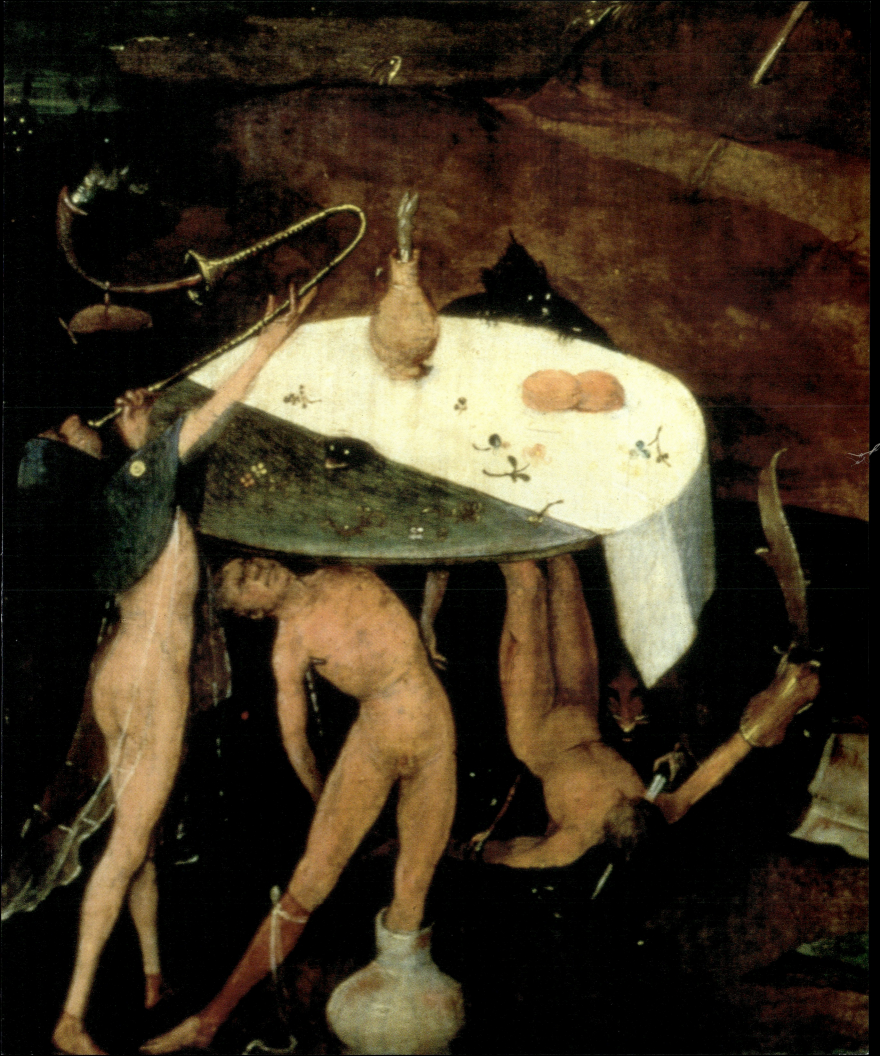

In 1613 a Dane painted this picture of an evidently merry evening. In the background the windowpanes are like bottle ends.

Glass

Nordic people never had any trouble procuring something to drink. Nor were they in want of something to drink from. Skulls, horns, mugs, fashioned from every thinkable material, all would serve the purpose, including these delicate objects, that were owned only by few: the glass.

In the mid 16th century the nobility were building great and the king even greater. This accomplishment included the ultimate innovation: window-panes of glass.

Glass had become less costly, so applying it in windows was affordable, and although it appeared uneven and greenish the sunlight, unbelievably, penetrated inside. As the window-panes took hold it made sense to cut down on imports and instead establish a domestic production that would also facilitate the making of drinking glasses.

The two Nordic kingdoms, the dual monarchy of Denmark-Norway and Sweden with included Finland both looked for expert guiding.

Venice being famous for its glass abounded in experts, but harsh reprisals awaited artists attempting to escape from the city-state.

Nevertheless a few but hardly the most talented braved it even to the far North. And a manufactory was established.

In Denmark it was centred around smelteries, that were put up in Skanderborg county. Here items such as bottles, retorts and plain drinking glasses were produced.

The making of glass, however, is enormously fuel consuming. A consignment of bottles would easily lay waste a small forest, and in the powerful seafaring nation such an onslaught raised concern. The fleet was touchy about a steady supply of wood, particularly of oak timber, so eventually the smelteries were forced to close down. The fleet's requirements were given higher priority.

The Swedes fared differently. They continued work under royal protection and with German assistance. As late as 1676 a stray Italian mendicant friar appeared. Following a period spent as a spiritual adviser at a smeltery in Amsterdam, he reported in Stockholm, introducing himself as Marquis Guagnini, a true master in the art of making glass. The concession was issued, and Kungsholm works was founded.

As was to be expected the false marquis failed to perform so the unmasking of his fraud followed, and he disappeared. But Kungsholm remained and with a new leadership it was to create some of the most distinguished glassware of the day.

A magnificent goblet from the Kungsholm works. Sweden abt.1690. Venetian style with Karl XI´s crowned monogram.

Hurling a glass through the air was considered a sign of friendship, especially if it had been emptied. When fashion prescribed one for each guest, hosts tended to choose wooden ones. Only they made little noise when thrown, so for a while heavy flying stone mugs took over.

Nothing, however, is like the ringing of glass – its crisp exciting jingle as it splinters in joyous stimulation of Man's inherent instinct for destruction. And now as windowpanes had been installed, guests in a festive mood might double the effect if they managed to hit the bull´s eye. Even royalty succumbed to the fun, as became apparent to the pharmacist of Bergen on the advent of the young Christian IV´s visit in 1599. Not a single window was spared.

By this time requirements for the Danish court amounted to four thousand glasses per year, and at the coronation in 1596 glasses were smashed with abandon.

The order comprised 20.000 small conical tumblers, 10.000 full size and 5.000 halfsize benndicken, a total of 35.000 pieces.

However it was the plain, non-decorated, if not to say mass-produced kind that coronation guests would handle. The magnificent goblet with matching lid only ventured its wandering down the table when sure hands were ready to receive it.

The ordinary drinking glass had become an object for festivities in the same category as fireworks. It was procured for and written off with the event.

The term "pasglas" indicates its function as a sort of measuring glass. Toothed groves divide this 14 inches high early 1600´s glass into six equal volumes. It is circular at the base, octagonal at the rim. One of the most popular and cheapest glasses of that time, it was meant be passed around.

Rosenholm was one of the Danish mansions to shoot up during the Renaissance. The rectangular complex of buildings was fully completed in 1570 and since then it has been held by the Rosenkranz family.

In 1960 and the following years the moat was dredged and on that occasion large numbers of mugs, kitchenware and other utensils were recovered, this glass being one of them.

Not just animated guests tossed things, the household, too, used the moat as a rubbish dump for worn-out material, so nobody knows if the glass was still intact when discarded.

FROM BREAD TO WHITE GOLD

Plates

The slice of bread – also known as the bread disk – prevailed well into the Nordic Renaissance. Besides it served a double purpose. After the meal the rich bread was given to the poor, unless one simply poured sugar and honey over it and had it as a dessert.

When in 1577 Elsinore celebrated the birth of Christian IV with royal attendance, the table was laid with bread disks, but at that time the plate proper had already appeared on the scene.

For some time tablets of wood were alternatively employed. Now these were turned and given depth so as to keep moisture in its place rather than spilling onto the table cloth. The shape was transferred to tin and later, among the wealthy, also to silver, not that one would have to give one to each. It was quite all right to have a couple of guests share a plate. After all it was a move forward from the common bowl.

The food in the Nordic countries was a phenomenon all its own. An Englishman marked it "the worst I have experienced", while another visitor focussed on the quantitative with his barrage: "They feed like swine."

November was the season for butchering most farm animals. The meat was salted, smoked or dried and after months in the brine or hanging from the ceiling it tended to develop a stale flavour to it. Here a kick from spices was needed.

Spices were immensely costly as long as they were to be carried on camel- or horseback - along the silk route. But then the Portuguese found the seaway to India whereupon entire shiploads called at European ports, making prices plummet.

Now Northerners ran amuck. Without the slightest sense of either quantity or composition they took to the exotics and heaped nauseating amounts of cinnamon, saffron, nutmeg, clove and pepper upon favourite dishes such as stuffed head of mutton or honey cooked ox-feet.

Turned wooden plates are used during a peasant wedding and are being dealt out by menservants. In the background the bride seems to thank the Lord for having been married off. To the right a monk and a nobleman are engaged in conversation.

On top of this came the drinking. The morning would start with large quantities of beer and the consumption grew as the day wore on.

The state of Denmark is best illustrated by an ordinance of 1593. To secure just reasonably sober witnesses, courts were decreed to sit no later than 8 am. The royal command aimed at nobles, townspeople and peasantry alike, so it did not distinguish between classes. But there were likely differences of circumstances under which a person got tight.

The poor managed with their home-brew, supplemented with the relatively novel dram, while the wealthier preferred Rhinewine, claret and heavy German beer.

According to the memoirs of 1692, by Molesworth, the English Ambassador to Denmark, cherry brandy also contributed to keeping up moisture level on these latitudes, where the vomiting tub was an indispensable piece of furniture even in the highest circles.

Each meal was preceded by grace. One prayer ended up with the words:: To His glory and to our gain / drink and dine we in His name.

While the crazed abuse of spices was a special Nordic feature, drinking was considerably more widespread. A dividing line existed somewhere between the far more controlled Latin Europe and the Germanic part, where excessive intake was considered a virtue in every honest man.

Charles Ogier was secretary to the French ambassador when he attended a royal wedding in Copenhagen in 1634. In view of the circumstances Ogier expressed his surprise with diplomatic delicacy: "Dining sites, bedrooms and halls were literally awash."

The art of painting spent little in the way of cosmetics on the side effects of general loose living.

*Faience from Faenza
16th century.*

*Two out of eighteen ornamental
plates of silver and amber,
Königsberg abt.1585. A present
to the King of Denmark.*

This particular lifestyle influenced the attitude with which Nordic courts regarded elegant plates: those made of faience.

Faience, to some extent, was a novelty by which a covering tin glaze over fired earthenware allowed the artist to unfurl his talent with motives ranging from the original Moorish inspiration to frivolous Italian erotica.

Faience was fragile, however, it all too easily broke with an unintended encounter with the floor, and here it was not just a matter of primitive drinking glasses, but nothing less than valuables.

Even in cultivated France things might go terribly wrong as exemplified by a banquet given by Cardinal de Birague in 1580, when the majority of 1000 splendid dishes ended in the dustbins. An indignant witness to the massacre described the lackeys as "born asses".

In the Nordic countries the condition of the guests coupled with the young attendants unsure gait made such happenings the rule rather than the exception. So to speak every object was sent flying, and since, all taken, there was a limit to how much even royalty would spend on animated spells, the faience for a while was kept at a distance.

The silversmith's stack of bills for mending fractures or hammering out dents was, after all, a lesser evil. At least the noble metal remained intact.

Bargaining for precious objects in the Far East.

Parallel to the refinement of faience another fully as exotic and far more distinguished beauty had emitted her siren call to the well-to-do. It was porcelain.

In 1514 the first shipment arrived in a Portuguese port as a simple ship's ballast. Before that a few pieces, it is true, had overcome the distance via the silk route, but as small curios only.

Six years later a regular import was in progress, and as porcelain fanned out across Europe it attracted wonder. It was more white than anything seen before, thinner, glossy, impregnable and of a hardness far exceeding that of the porous faience. As the amazement subsided it appeared obvious just to go ahead and copy it's qualities.

Attempts to duplicate, however, failed over and over, and decades lapsed into half and full centuries. Meanwhile the myth of "white gold" gained momentum.

Far from all ships reached their destination, many went down with cargo and all. One was the Dutch Geldermalsen that sank in 1751 off the coast of Java. The wreckage was salvaged some twenty years ago, and divers photographed the porcelain in its bed on the bottom of the sea.

There is a sea-snail by the name of Porcella, meaning little pig. According to legend it was Marco Polo who, inspired by its glossy shell, gave its name to the newly discovered China ware. The creature is now nick named porcelain snail. But after all the small mollusk was first.

THE NORDIC TABLE

"...not to lick your fingers, spit on the plate, blow your nose in the table cloth, nor gulp like animals."

Ordinance of 1624 for young officers at the Austrian court.

Epoch of Splendour

Absolutism and Behaviour

By the time Renaissance merged into Baroque daily life had changed radically. Tile and iron stoves would take care of heating without spewing fumes or soot. Fur coats were slipped off indoors, leather stockings had been replaced by wool, cotton or silk, and even during shivering midwinter frost laces, embroidery and starched collars were given justice.

Master and mistress no longer shared the table with the servants now their body heat was no longer needed. The once so intimate relationship in the household gradually faded away as preparing of the meals was banished to the cellar and so made invisible.

Dining was given respectable conditions among people of distinction. Eating now took place under lofty ceilings and in generous space, and as chairs completely took over the function of benches, greater comfort resulted.

The Baroque introduced manners to the Nordic countries. You no longer had to add noise to hilarity, and use of the vomiting tub declined. When a Danish royal lunch given in 1655 proceeded entirely without embarrassing incidents, the Spanish ambassador ascribed the credit for such civilised behaviour to the German born queen Sofie Amalie. She was said to have emphatically disapproved of "Nordic savagery".

It is estimated that porcelain first appeared in Denmark at the beginning of the 17th century, evidenced mainly by one still existing bowl. However travelling was practised with admirable fervour, and large quantities of goods passed though Øresund by ship, so single pieces could well have appeared at an earlier date.

But not until the Baroque, when tableware gradually lost its function as a source of projectiles, did the inclination to lay tables with porcelain become evident.

A table splendidly laid during absolutism. As a matter of course precious metal is displayed. In the middle is a "surtout", a centrepiece for salt, sugar, spices, oil and other essentials. Knives have retained their pointed blades. Glasses are not in evidence, but lined up at a sideboard. There they are filled and brought back to each guest. Folds in the table cloth indicated that it came fresh from the linen room. To accentuate the point a special damask press was put to use.

Everything was subordinated the strict rules of aesthetics. This too included stoves. They were not just to emit heat, but they must also appear pleasing to the eye not to interfere with the beauty of the room.

Most iron stoves were cast in Norway, many of them featuring stylish reliefs on their sides. In certain cases they were furnished with a superstructure of faience.

Illumination, too, was subject to change. On the advent of the Baroque the burning of wax-candles escalated immensely in well-to-do houses. Indeed, on festive occasions candles might involve expenses in the same order as those of all the servings combined.

Now they shone and the light flashed from the profusion of prisms in chandeliers and girandola while novel large mirrors lavishly multiplied the effect.

One of the earliest Nordic crystal chandeliers. The style is Venetian, but it was made in Stockholm in the 1670´s.

A so-called procelain stove. The lower part is Norwegian and the iron sides from 1724 bear the double portrait of Frederik IV and his queen Anne Sophie Reventlow.

The upper part is a yet unsolved puzzle. It could be Danish, although the yellowish colour does point at a North German or, more likely, Frisian origin.

THE NORDIC TABLE

Drinking Hot

By the end of the 17th century hot beverages made their entry onto the European scene. Coffee with its roots in the Middle East and tea from China were first sold by pharmacists as medicine, the former as a laxative, the latter was considered effectual against swellings and cramps.

The new beverages took hold and spread as stimuli in their own right, and the insulating porcelain protected the fingers from getting burnt.

Coffee-houses shot up all over London, and the citizenry of Holland were on the verge of going amuck, and the sea captain Cornelis Bontecoe recommended up to two hundred daily cups of tea, in 1696 "Haagische Mercurius" noted that "his joints rattled like castanets".

In Denmark the new craze was adapted in a more controlled manner. As for the broad countryside with peasants caught in an economic deroute the old faithful acquaintances, homebrew and dram, stood their ground. In contrast tea and coffee invaded the better situated circles. The same is true of cocoa which had initiated its European career in the shape of little brown loaves, later to be turned fluid under the name of chocolate.

So the new fashion developed into a pleasure and pastime for the upper classes, who paid visits to each other and would gladly spend on necessary equipment including special jugs. From here it filtered down to those less wealthy city dwellers who were eager to handle what a contem-

porary writer Ludvig Holberg called a "bowl" of coffee. The cup, the one with a handle, was still to come.

English tea drinkers.

Porcelain had become an article for daily use. But it still had to travel the long treacherous way south of Malaya, south of India, south of Africa and finally from there up to European ports.

In Persuit of the White Gold

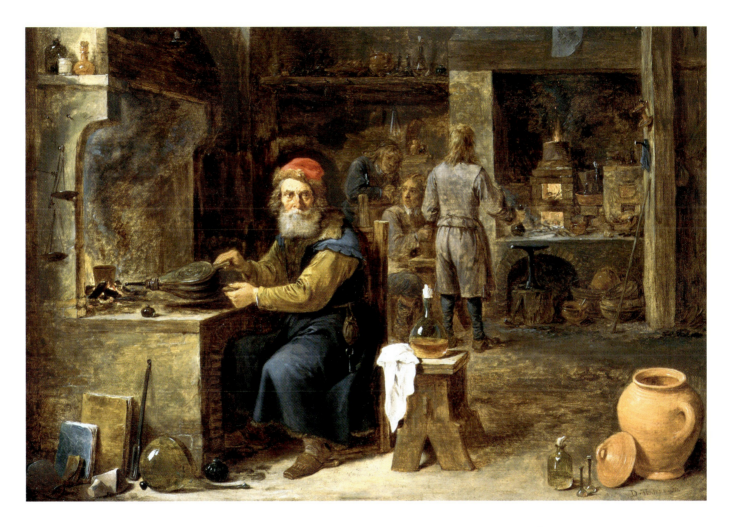

An alchemist in his workshop.

Almost two centuries had elapsed with no real progress in the search for the secret of the making of porcelain. Hardness was lacking, and so it went on.

It galled every European power to see an abundance of good genuine silver being sent off solely because they failed to solve the riddle of manufacturing procedures.

To be able to establish a production of his own would be of immense benefit for a ruler as well as for his country.

Expectations of princely favour have always aroused the quickwitted. In this case swindlers and aristocrats, academies and chemists besides those alchemists who, throughout historic times have striven to produce that other gold, the precious metal. Many died during experiments involving toxic agents and most of them slipped into oblivion.

Johan Friederich Böttger was Prussian by birth and trained as a pharmacist. With lavish promises of mastering the making of gold from lead he had relieved his king of considerable means, then he vanished. Before disappearing, however, he managed to produce something that looked much like gold, and that fact attracted too much attention for his comfort.

Birds of Böttkers breed were not allowed to flutter about for long, and his flight from one ruler sent him headlong into the arms of another.

August the Strong, Elector of Saxony and King of Poland promoted beauty in all its forms and shades but first of all he was obsessed with porcelain.

The king afforded shelter for Böttger by locking him up. Conditions were convenient, though, with abundant funds, roomy quarters and servants to look after every need. There was a laboratory with an unlimited number of assistants at his service, all aimed at the one and only objective: to deliver the precious metal.

Time went by and nothing happened. Whenever Böttger attempted to sneak away he would face soldiers ready to escort him back.

King August must have sensed that this wild, unruly and seedy pharmacist was not altogether devoid of talent. Was he incapable of delivering one kind of gold, he would have to make up for it by producing the other, the white gold i.e. porcelain. Such was the royal order.

August the Strong in all his might reproduced in red porcelain.

Meissen´s version of the Danish king was quite differently modest in its presentation. It amounted to a portrait of his Majesty when young, his profile plaited with gold.

Böttger sourly responded by pinning a note on his door reading: "Alchemist turned potter".

Bohemian Count von Tschirnhaus had for a long time served King August for the very same purpose, and co-operation was established between the two. While the count concentrated on the task of achieving the 1300 degrees centigrade necessary to obtain hardness, Böttger went in search of a variety of clay that would endure the heat without cracking.

Gradually they made headway. Experiments with kaolin mixed with feldspar proved successful and on January 15th 1708, following twelve hours of firing, the first piece of European porcelain was taken from the kiln.

August rubbed his hands. To be sure

Leipzig was far more close to European buyers than were Canton and the trading station of Macao. He issued a decree for establishing the Royal Saxon Porcelain Manufactury.

As part of a major educational journey Danish Frederik IV visited Saxony the following year. The cordial reception included a visit to the palace of Oranienburg outside Berlin. Here mirrors allowed the inspection of porcelain from all angles, that is to say the Chinese porcelain. Of the remaining story King August never uttered a word.

In 1710 the news was sprung. The Leipzig fair opened to reveal a European product nobody had seen before.

Red porcelain it was named from its coloration and was if anything even thinner and harder than the Chinese. Besides it could be cut as though it were glass.

Covered tureen from Meissen with Chinese decoration. 1730-35.

The Danish king's response to this news is not known, but we do know precisely what his European colleges went about: they sent spies.

At this time Tschirnhaus had already died and Böttger sat isolated from the outside world working on the completion of the white porcelain that was ready for sale in 1713. But he too, the gifted troublemaker, was denied the chance to enjoy his triumph for long.

Böttger was given his freedom and in addition the position as manager of the factory. He did not own the gift of leadership, so it was only after his death a few years later that production really progressed.

His legacy, however, was to be nothing less than the world famous Meissen porcelain. King August duly recognised the achievement to the extent of making an entire palace for his colossal collection of porcelain both Chinese and his own produce. Here the cabinets lacked the space required.

When spies failed to get hold of the master they went for his co-workers instead. A number of them were open to bribery; they contributed to a start-up up in Vienna in 1720. A few of them strayed on to Venice where the next manufactory was established, and by 1770 the number of production sites had attained about fifty.

The first Chinaman to visit Sweden. On July 20th 1786 the Chinese merchant Choi A-fuk arrived in Gothenburg as the guest of Swedish shipowner Oluf Linddahl. On that occasion A-fuk met Baron de Geer and his wife Aurora. He is here seen with the flirtatious Aurora and a slightly worried Lindahl.

China in the North

The Portuguese were denied their continued dominance of the Far Eastern trade. Others followed: Holland, England soon also Denmark and eventually Sweden.

Shipload upon shipload called at European ports with their cargoes of lacquered works, silk and embroidery, glass paintings, and, funds permitting, entire rooms were renovated and arranged to comply with the passion for things oriental.

The development of European porcelain moved a considerable proportion of the purchases to Leipzig, Berlin etc., but this did not bring an end to imports from the Far East.

A steadily growing demand for the inexpensive blue and white porcelain was supplied largely from overseas. Besides many customers willingly waited for years to get their pre-ordered products with personally selected colours, patterns, initials or coats of arms.

As a part of their wages crew members according to rank were allowed a number of cubic feet in the hold for their own purchases.

These were sold on their return to European ports – if they had the good fortune to survive the voyage.

Four dissimilar fruit plates from the set.

Chinese export porcelain with decorations in red and gold from late 18th century. The style bears witness to the European fashion of that time, but it is hardly custom-made work. More likely it was brought home by a sea captain or mate.

The remarkable tableware belongs to a Danish family. For an unknown number of years it lay unnoticed in a crate relegated to a Zealand wash house. It was not discovered until recent time, but the hideout spared the treasure from being split among heirs or partially sold out. So many pieces being kept together is a rare occurrence.

Glass From Norway

Up through the 18th century the citizenry enjoyed a steadily improving economy, which allowed for new consumer habits. The drinking glass won life expectancy. It was ment for keeps and repeated use. The stemmed glass had become fashionable, and some of the noblest of that time were to be created in Norway.

The centre of gravity for glassmaking had moved. Venice no longer controlled the market while Bohemia had become predominant and England too was much in evidence.

Since Denmark suffered a shortage of wood the idea of transferring the manufacture to heavily forested Norway seemed obvious. Upon the order of King Christian VI the first Norwegian glassworks was founded at Nøstetangen near Hokksund in 1741, and German glass-blowers were sent for. They were responsible for the German names subsequently given to several models. The outcome displayed grace and harmony even if transparency was slightly hazy and shapes perhaps on the heavy side.

Close ties existed between Norway and England. The connecting route was from coast to coast, encouraging a bustling exchange of goods, and in 1775 James Keith, an English expert on glass, was successfully invited to Norway.

Keith knew his trade inside out. The glasses were given lightness and became stylish, so much the more when cut by Köhler, the famous engraver.

Illustrated inventories indicate that in a period of ten years the number of models increased from modest 23 to a choice of 75. The assortment covered all price brackets and also included decanters, as these became fashionable in wealthy homes.

A table in Norway. The porcelain is Chinese Famille Rose and
flowers are arranged in goblets with their lids put next to them.
But it is the largest of the glasses that makes the picture remarkable.
They are the produce of Nøstetangen.
This home is one of only two or three in the world to have
preserved the glasses that were specially ordered from this works
more than two hundred years ago.

It was here in the coastal region of Norway, where the Vestfoss river empties into the Drammen, the famous glasses came into being.

Glasses in greatest demand included those with red, blue or yellow enamel spirals adorning the stem or with patterns that could be obtained by applying air.

According to customers wishes, the engraver would cut monograms, coats of arms, perhaps a few maxims or just loving words.

But even Nøstentangen ran into fuel problems. In 1779 the entire production had to be integrated into Hurdal, another great Norwegian glass-works.

Postmaster Pind of Larvik, Norway, was, like many a bourgeois of that time, a man of means. He had portraits. made of himself and the whole family sitting by a table engraved in glass. The table is laid with drinking glass but it is the patriarch's privilege to hold the precious goblet in his hand.

Nøstetangen glass from abt.1770 with engravings by Köhler. On the back is an inscription reading: "Put a finger on my hole or I shall piss you drunk". In front a mermaid is holding a spray in her hands. Her sex is pierced, so the ensuing hole must be covered to prevent wine from spilling.

The nautical lady has been supplied with twin tails for the occasion.

The Grand Royal Table

Dominance seeks prominence, and in no century did splendour, luxury and refinement unfold to such extent as that of the 18th century. Europe – and also Denmark – was influenced by French autocracy, by French language and culture, and as for the courts they scrupolously followed even the slightest modification of fashion in Versailles.

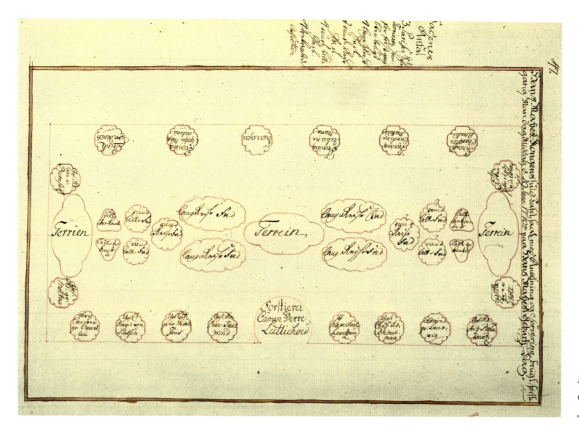

On January 29. 1770, a royal table was laid at the castle of Christiansborg in Copenhagen. The occasion was Christian VII´s 21-year birthday, and the hour was 2.30 pm as customary for such events.

A plan of this table has been preserved. It shows placement and the complete presentation and decoration as laid down in "Service à la française":

The Table Decker of that era could be likened with the garden landscaper. While the latter fashioned his own cosmetic variety of nature´s profiles by cutting trees and shrubs the former would exercise his creativity on the basis of the white tablecloth. The importance of symmetry and harmony was exactly the same.

The same table reconstructed at Christian VII´s Palace, Amalienborg. If the overall impression appears shallow it is due in part to the absence of glasses and partly to the daylight rendering candles superfluous.

It was customary to place a so-called plateau in the middle of the table. It consisted of a wooden plate resting on short legs, and it had a cover of reflecting glass rimmed with either silver or gilt bronze. Upon the plateau fine objects such as figurines or even a romantic landscape was arranged.

Another possibility was a centrepiece with salt, sugar, oils, spices and other essentials. Fresh flowers, on the other hand, were seldom looked upon with favour, those of wax or porcelain being preferred. Should fresh flowers neverthe-

less appear, they would be fixed with wires. The table plan in question placed a splendid tureen as a centre-piece, supplemented by one at either end, while bowls and dishes were arranged in a carefully balanced pattern. Spices and accessories surrounded each cover and so made up their own little universe.

For royal persons everything was of gold. Besides spoon, fork and knife the set also included a spicebox and an eggcup. In addition, there was a new implement having in one end an egg spoon, in the other a marrow knife.

As already mentioned glasses would rest on the sideboards, where wine was poured. When emptied they were expediently brought back for washing and refilling.

Service was at the highest level. One chamberlain would carve while other high-ranking nobles were responsible solely for the needs of royalty.

Young pages took care of the remaining diners.

The food awaited the guests before they were seated. Here was the first menu, in this case a matter of seventeen dishes. Everyone could then ask for whatever was the most tempting and so compose his or her own menu. With this completed the table was cleared and the second and last set was brought in.

The royal cover from the same reconstruction. Cutlery is in gold, To the left of the plate the new elongated utensil, in one end egg spoon, in the other a marrow knife.

Left: J. F Struensee 1737-72. The german physician-in-ordinary for the lunatic king. He rose to become head of the king´s goverment and the queen's lover.

Right: Caroline Mathilde 1751-75, English princess, Danish queen.

Two barrel-shaped mustard jars, the work of Jørgen Nielsen Lind, 1740-50. The jars are still in daily use by the Danish royal family.

At the royal banquet of January, 1770, the table plan shows the presence of several Queens. Two of them are of particular interest: the king's stepmother Juliane Marie, who was his father's second wife, and his spouse Caroline Mathilde.

Formal records report on arrangement and placement, but they fall short of offering hints at the atmosphere during the banquet, specifically that between the two royal ladies.

Juliane Marie was an energetic lady of German background, Caroline Mathilde was the well-bred daughter of nature loving England and devoid of any idea of state or social matters or even of the marriage that she had entered at the age of 15.

The king was a lunatic, while the court physician was gifted, charming and ambitious. On just this occasion relations between queen and physician had approached the point of alarming intimacy.

On November 22, 1771, Caroline Mathilde set out from the castle of Hirschholm. She and a handful of friends went for an outing in the romantic landscape of northern Zealand. In her loneliness she had collected a group of confidantes and together they enjoyed the fresh air as was customary for her during adolescense.

The Queen´s love of outdoor life also influenced her choice of food. The menu was composed exclusively of cold servings such as oysters, fish and salads. Nature, however, was present in more than one sense, and Struensee was the pathfinder when the party ventured into uncharted territory.

Nine weeks later, on January 17, 1772, the coup d´etat was upon them. The dowager queen was not really responsible for the initiative, but she did play a major role once the drama was set in motion.

Caroline Mathilde and her lover were taken into custody. The young queen was eventually exiled, and Struensee ended his days on the scaffold under circumstances so bestial that even the toughest Europeans were shaken.

The Lord Steward's only comment to the coup was his dry entry: The cold servings are cancelled and henceforth non-existent".

One of the magnificent tureens that was used at the royal table.

Under the Rose

In 1711the French artist le Coffre painted a joyous going-on in the Rose at Frederiksberg Castle.

Sideboards for pouring could have a number of tiers, but here it is a matter of just two. At the upper silver is at display while the lower one functions much as a bar for everyone's free convenience.

Princely houses had a hall for courtiers, where everybody could engage in festivities, in drinking and exchange of indiscreet comments, even those involving royal persons.

These premises in time became known as The Rose, that term having evolved from Latin sub rosa. Dining under the rose was tantamount to a free flow of the most confidential matter, all on one condition though: none of it was to escape into the outside world.

Stockholm New Year's Day 1779

Since the day of the Sun King courtiers carefully watched royalty`s every step from morning till night. Thus the privileged in France could witness the particular ceremonial attached to "lever" and "coucher", in other words when the king rose and again when he went to bed. Likewise it was considered an exquisite honour to be present at his meals.

When, in 1771, Gustav III ascended the throne, the conquering of Skåne from Denmark had long bestowed upon Sweden the leading position as the great power of Scandinavia. This was evident both in military strength and in culture.

The francophile king influenced the ways and taste of his people more than any other ruler. The particular style became known as the Gustavian and was the happy alliance between French abundance and Swedish grace. Colours are light, marble had given way to painted decoration, and high windows open to the crisp Nordic light.

On New Year's day, 1779, the court, supplemented with select members of government and the diplomatic corps were present at Gustav III´s supper at the Stockholm Palace. Thirteen years later Gustav III was murdered at the hands of nobles during a fancy dress ball at the castle.

It happened a year before the absolute monarch above all others, Louis XVI, was decapitated before the eyes of the mob at Place de la Concorde, Paris.

The king is sitting with his two brothers at his right side. At the king´s left his queen, his sister-in-law and his sister. In the foreground the Lord Camberlain conducts the proceedings.. Stools are reserved for the ministers` wives and ladies of the corps diplomatique, while everybody else must watch the dining standing. The atmosphere appears relaxed. Conversations are flowing.

Tureen in gold and silver, which was in Gustav III´s possession.

Placing the Table

The table had always been movable. Originally it consisted of planks laid on trestles. This simplicity made it easy to remove when musicians struck up for dancing. Nevertheless through poverty and festivities alike the table was the foundation of life. In the name of the Lord it supported the food.

During the long course of evolution, however, that real prime performer

was neglected. It is true that its colonies made mahogany available to the English, who at this time introduced fine dining room furniture with polished surfaces. But on the continent nobody paid any attention to the looks of the table.

In larger houses, the premises for setting up meals were selected according to the occasion and the instant mood and requirement of the master and the mis-

The Hermitage in the deer park north of Copenhagen. One of the asylums in which the table could be hoisted from the kitchen.

tress of the house. So it had been reduced to a sort of vagabonding platform that supported the finery. Only in one environment did the table maintain its safe location: the hermitage.

Royalty spent their day facing a crowd of courtiers, officials, ambassadors and people of all description seeking audience. On this background the idea of the hermitage was conceived. They were modest size buildings with room enough for a few intimates.

Even servants could have sensitive ears, so in some of these hermitages the table would be prepared in the cellar and, with all dishes ready, be hoisted up through the floor by means of an ingenious mechanism.

The Danish mathematician and inventor Ole Rømer had been responsible for some of the engineering involved in the fountains of Versailles and also became the architect of cleverly constructed elevating tables. The first of his arrangements proved more durable than the last.

Hermitage by Fredensborg castle. Fishing and sailing in viking ships are going on and falling into the water too.

Splendour had attained its zenith, but without hygiene following suit, and this was not a specific Nordic feature. It crawled and crept under wigs and corsets from Stockholm to Madrid, and even the most distinguished had their beds put on stilts to prevent rats from invading the beddings.

15-year old Erik von Høgh was a page at the court of the now demolished Hirschholm palace. Letters he sent to "beloved Mama" make moving reading. He was pent up in his tight tunic and rigid shoes. He wrestled with dishes and yearned for his Mariager home with "Lars the gamekeeper and the bailiff, Lene and old Talle".

But he had all his eyes about him on his solitary wanderings in the early morning hours, "since owing to bed bugs I could not sleep. It is a magnificent palace". Erik von Høgh describes his royal masters wisely and with humour. But since the little bunch of letters came to an end in 1752, we unfortunately are not told of his encounter with Queen Juliane Marie who arrived shortly after.

Juliane Marie was deeply engaged in art and culture and her initiative would involve more than just participating in a coup d'etat. The Salon of her ladies-in-waiting at Fredensborg castle is preserved. It testifies to exquisite taste. And to her goes the credit for the establishment of the Royal Copenhagen Porcelain Factory.

*"Good meals are much more rare
than good women. And far more piquant."*

Brillat-Savarin.

The Realm of Plants

Swedish Attempts

The first attempts to produce porcelain were made in Denmark and Sweden during the 1720´s.

Assistance was willingly offered by many, including some of those from Böttger´s old team, who were still roaming about. But their stay would prove as brief as achievements were meagre.

In the case of Sweden, however one individual singled out from the bunch of hopeful amateurs: the former court dentist, German born Johan Ludwig Ehrenreich.

Teeth made of porcelain had become fashionable, but apart from a knowledge of this limited field, Ehrenreich´s chemical experience was at best diffuse. His strong points were his sense of the artistic and – no less important - an ability to formulate his ideas.

Selecting his words carefully he, in an application of 1758, emphasised the tremendous amount of money that went to waste in the hands of oriental merchants as well as on the bottom of the high seas.

Nothing could be more Swedish than the Gripsholm tableware from the end of the 18th century, It was nevertheless commisioned work manufactured in China.

As a result permission to start up a production was granted, and the property of Marieberg was acquired for that purpose.

The first firings were carried out on May 14, 1759, and on the night of June 1st another attempt was made. This time the whole works went up in flames.

Marieberg was rebuilt but managed only to manufacture faience and, as earnings were failing, Ehrenreich had to retire in 1766.

The Swedish experiments continued. Marieberg employed Jacob Dortu, a Berlin educated porcelain painter. Dortu did not affect Marieberg artistically, but he was the man who knew about the technology behind the real thing, hard porcelain.

Swedish subsoil contained no kaolin, so Dortu is believed to have procured that essential type of clay through connections in Prussia. Dortu made off in 1777, possibly because the inventory stock was exhausted. As for his expert knowledge he took it with him.

The 18th century was the great heyday of European porcelain. That was the time when Meissen, Fürstenberg and other producers came into being. In Sweden it all amounted to just one year combined, and that was the end of it.

Danish Entry

Queen Juliane Marie was the daughter of Carl, Duke of Braunschweig. The duke had opened the first German manufactory of porcelain since Meissen, so the Queen knew not only the economic impact but also its cultural significance for a country's international reputation.

At the age of 23 she had been married to Frederik V, becomming his second queen. His first wife had already given birth to the heir to the throne, the later Christian VII, the lunatic king.

Juliane Marie´s position was not an easy one. In reality she was just a substitute as a wife, as a mother and as a queen. Nor did she ever win popularity, and the coup d´etat contributed to the gloomy shadows that were cast upon her name during her lifetime as well as after her death.

As a dowager queen, however, in 1775 she took a step for which the nation ought to be deeply indebted to her. While others were reluctant, she bought shares in the ailing little Copenhagen business "The Danish Porcelain Fabrique" belonging to a chemist by the name of Heinrich Müller.

Heinrich Müller was born in Copenhagen. Like Böttger he was a pharmacist by education, and to this he had added studies of metallurgy in both Sweden and Norway.

Müller held the neccesary qualifications, and by this time kaolin had been located on the Danish island of Bornholm.

Queen Juliane Marie

The factory in Købmagergade, Copenhagen.

In 1773 he was awarded a licence to try his hand at the production of porcelain.

As opposed to Böttger´s case Müller was not locked up, but then he had to pay expenses out of his own pocket.

Some of the firings were successful, others went wrong, and as problems arose the dowager queen stepped forward and came to his rescue.

This was not sufficient, though. Production proceeded to a point, but the quality was rather common and additional funds were needed. In 1779 the crown assumed full responsibilities for finances. At this time the mad king's authority was de facto delegated to the government and Juliane Marie.

They were the real rulers, and "The Royal Copenhagen Porcelain Factory" became a reality. Naturally problems did not just evaporate overnight, nevertheless spectacular progress became evident both technically and as regards artistic quality.

Often patterns were influenced by great masters abroad. The bulk was dominated by dinner services, primarily the blue-white variety that appealed to a broad selection of consumers, and the sale was supported by a ban on most import.

Examples of very independent works did occur such as a series of vases produced 1789. They won the honour of being mentioned in a newspaper. The factory's dinner service of international fame, though, indirectly owes its creation to a Swede.

Father of Botany

Carl von Linné was born in the southern Swedish province of Småland 1707. He was the son of a minister and would often be named the most famous of all Swedes.

As a child Linné was far too occupied with his observations in forest and field to bother much about his schoolwork. All the same he managed to achieve his A-level and even a medical doctorate, but it was within the realm of plants he would scale the heights.

In this field his studies reached from Lapland to Skåne. Furthermore he travelled in France, England, Germany and the Netherlands. Swedish authorities vainly sent him to look for clay and plants that could be used in the production and coloration of porcelain.

By coincidence Heinrich Müller, the founder of Danish porcelain, used to be one of Linné´s students in Uppsala. So it could be argued that a small fraction of the credit should rightly be attributed to the professor.

Furiously hard working Linné was ennobled for his ground breaking work. Specifically his studies of the reproductive structures in plants led to a whole new system of classification and to the introduction of a nomenclature by which the first name indicates the family and the second the name of the species.

With some justification it has been said: God created. Linné organised. Nor was he devoid of self-esteem, describing himself as a person, who would be: "in the highest degree averse to everything that bore the appearance of pride."

In Denmark his efforts gave inspiration to the colossal set of books "Flora Danica" with its hand coloured copper prints featuring the wild flora of the kingdoms from Holstein to North Cape. Publishing was begun in 1761 and continued up until 1883.

Carl von Linné

Despite his prolonged stay in Holland
Linné never spent a word on the reputed
flower paintings of the country. Certainly
the models were a long way from
genuine uncultivated nature.

Except at the table flowers were adored
everywhere and that was particularly true
of the tulip.

   The tulip was just a humble plant with a
habitat in Turkey and eastward when it
came into the hands of the industrious
Dutch breeders.

   As one hybrid was succeded by the next
over and over, their heads swelled and
petals turned striped, flamed and frayed.
Eventually the Dutch tulip became the
great export article.

   Bulbs entered the world market as prices
soared. The most costly was Semper
Augustus as seen to the right. One bulb
of this variety might bring as much as the
value of two average houses.

   Then the marked collapsed. It was to be the
first and only crack in the field of tulip bulb
business..

   The flowers shot up again, though, and
artists continued painting them even if, as
already mentioned, they did not meet the
approval of the father of botany. For as
Linné made order in God´s creation, the
Dutch transformed it.

Flora Danica

On August 28. 1770 a messenger received the remarkably handsome pay of four Thalers for transporting the volumes of "Flora Danica" from the royal librarian at Christiansborg Castle to the porcelain factory in Købmagergade.

Underlying this little incident was a royal order to create one of history's greatest dinner services.

Unfortunately no further documentation can be found. Normally the administration working for the absolute monarchs would enter every penny into its accounts down to the pay for a glass of beer given to a sick worker.

Here, however, in a matter of creating the unique, the information goes no further than these four Thalers. A file of great volume must simply have been lost.

Even if documents are missing, all evidence supports the assumption that Flora Danica was foreseen as a gift to Catharina the Great of Russia.

At that time diplomatic ties between the two countries had cooled down. An alliance obliged Denmark to attack Sweden, but the ensuing Danish campaign came to nothing more than a half-hearted raid into the Swedish province of Bohuslän, embarrassingly dubbed "The Cowberry War":

The Zarina, in other words, must be appeased, and her adoration of both porcelain and botany were well known.

The plant, Linnaea Borealiis, as depicted in the book version of Flora Danica. It was Linné´s favourite flower and as such named after himself.

Plate for crème cups from the
original Flora Danice service.
The ornamentation illustrates
Datura Stramonium, Thorn Apple.

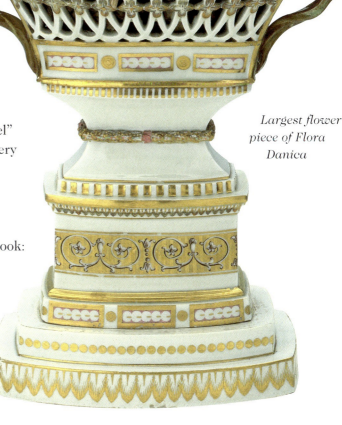

*Largest flower
piece of Flora
Danica*

The French archi-
tect Nicolas-Henri
Jardin brought classi-
cism to Denmark.

This style was inspired by
the Antique, it supplanted the capri-
cious, asymmetrical Rococo and marked architecture, furniture as well as
porcelain.

The new look is seen in the "perlestel"
from 1783, and the moulds from this very
service were selected for Flora Danica
when productions started.

The German painter J.C Bayer had
among other merits drawn favourable
attention with his illustrations for the book:
"Blissful country-side hours of repose,
spent in the company of mushrooms
in Denmark". He was given respon-
sibility for the decorations.

Bayer's task was of formidable
proportions. Not only did he
personally do most of the painting, which ultimately ruined his
eyesight. He was also called upon to transfer motifs from their initial rectangles to the
curving shapes of plates and tureens and this with every single stalk or pod preserved.

The printed version of Flora Danica was a work of science, but the same is true of the
porcelain. Botanical accuracy was given higher priority than decorative effect. It was a
matter of painstaking reproduction of nature and not just neat roses and violets. We are
invited to the very depths among roots, mosses and fungi. The golden rim was typical of
the era, but the motifs are timeless nature itself.

On the completion of the service the Zarina had already died so the Danish royal house kept it in their possession. Out of the original eighteen hundred pieces meant for a
hundred seating, more than fifteen hundred are preserved to this day, and on notable
occasions Flora Danica will still adorn the royal table.

The heavily populated quarter surrounding the Church of Our Lady was the main target of the bombardment in 1807. Here it is seen from a position just behind the factory.

The masterpiece was handed over to Christian VII in 1802. The year before the citizens of Copenhagen had crowded the city walls to watch admiral Nelson´s unannounced visit to the harbour of the capital.

Six years later the situation was at a far more sinister level. A new English attack made a devastating assault on the Danish fleet as well as on the capital itself. As firebombs fell on the city the porcelain factory got its share and was hit in the attic, where many of the moulds were kept.

Queen Alexandra in her coronation dress. She was then close to sixty.

THE NORDIC TABLE

*The battle of Copenhagen April 2. 1801
commemorated on a punch bowl and
given to the many heroes of the day.*

The bridal couple were Alexandra of
Denmark and the Prince of Wales, son of
Queen Victoria. In other words the Danish
princess was the Queen-to-be of the
people, who once scorched her capital.

Flora Danica, it was resolved, must be
revived and presended to the distinguished
couple. By some miracle most of its
moulds were found to have survived the
fire, only the decorations caused concern
among the ladies.

The time was 1862, the culmination of
Victorianism. A princess of the blood could
not possibly be exposed to the encounter
with plant roots beneath her soufflé nor face
fungi and similar decay at the bottom of a
tureen. Of course nature was captivating,
but only when carefully screened.

Luckily it was decided to preserve the
scientific point of origin, but a choise was
made from among the prints, while focus
was directed towards the gracious and the
unquestionably most beautiful.

The green colour was of concern. In the
realm of plants shades of green are naturally paramount. The first Flora Danica
appeared with copper based paints, which
lent a metallic richness to the hue. From
now on this was replaced by a chromium
compound that produced softer shades and
so conformed with contemporary taste for
the graceful.

The Flora Danica that can be seen at
Sandringham was the service number two.
It comprised 765 pieces corresponding to
the laying of 60 covers. Since then the
service has been in continuous production.

The end of the Napoleonic wars changed
the borders of Scandinavia. Sweden lost
Finland to Russia but instead took over
Norway, where hunger and distress had
extracted the war's heaviest toll from the
population. A margin for table decorations
no longer existed. Now it was a matter of
providing food.

As years went by the Royal Copenhagen
Porcelain Factory had become a sedate,
middle-aged concern with obvious shortcomings as to imagination and innovation.
The assortment consisted only of the
familiar and well established. Of course
there was Flora Danica, but the one and
only service belonged to the king, and to
resume production was unthinkable. Then
a group of Danish ladies were in want of an
idea for a wedding present.

Today Flora Danica is the only one of the 18th century´s magnificent dinner services currently produced and therefore the most expensive worldwide.

Every painter has years of training behind him, and working procedures are precisely as when the very first items came into being.

Firings are carried out with full regard to the original formula, and the gilded pearl pattern along rims is still eighteen carat.

Every decoration is shaped and assembled by hand, using knives, brushes and needles.

Motifs are painted freehand from the original prints, and a single object may require as many as six firings in a kiln. Closing the procedure the artist applies his initials together with the plant's Latin name written in the handwriting that prevailed when Flora Danica was first set off by messenger that August day in 1790.

The table is laid with the Flora Danica of today. The surrounding room, however, has remained untouched for more than two hundred years.

Both glasses and decanters are Norwegian Nøstetangen from the 18th century. Knives are of comparable seniority with the original pointed iron preserved. Spoon and fork for dessert conform to the fashion of that time with handles of porcelain matching the tableware. Salt-cellars are far more recent, and pepper mills modern Bernadotte design from Georg Jensen. The small jars have always been intended for butter, while the idea of salad plates is of a later date.

"At the full bloom the decay begins."

Japanese proverb.

Victorianism

Weight and Volume

The 19th century ment the advance of the bourgeoisie and mass production, those being the watchwords of the era.

When, in the 1840´s, machinery spewed out textiles it heralded Victorianism. An orgy in plush, doorcurtains and draperies closed in with a confusion of styles, a parade of photos, of palms and the influx of bric-a-brac. Repose for the eye was a taboo. It could never be too crowded.

When 1814-15 the Vienna congress settled the estate left by Napoleonic wars it was time to celebrate as well, and here the Russian delegates brought a new custom. At the Russian table every guest was served individually having just one course at a time, and the servings were not brought in until everybody had taken their seats.

"Service à la Russe" gained a footing first in the highest classes, while the increasingly self-confident bourgeoisie chose their own more conservative way.

By now the table had got its fixed position in the family dining room, and after decades this group finally gave in to the new style. The strictly symmetrical composition of plates and tureens slowly disappeared and something else had to be introduced to cover the blank spaces.

Fresh flowers seemed an obvious compensation as were novelties like the finger bowl of the late Empire and the presentation plate, not to forget the menu card.

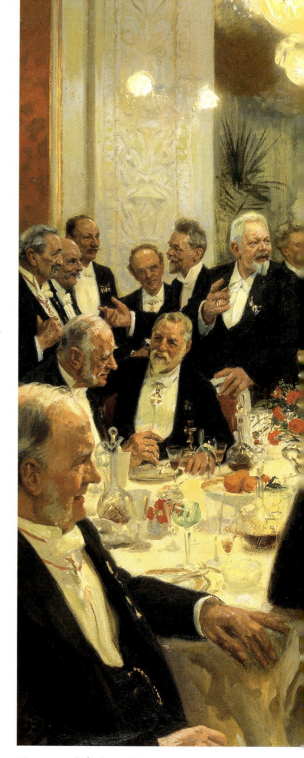

No guests left the table hungry or thirsty.

So far it had been possible to organise one's appetite and make choices out of desire and need. Now no one knew what or how much was in store ahead. And since, at all times, it was bad manners not to finish the plate, a little card was laid before every two diners. On this courses and wines were listed in orderly columns written, as they were in neat handwriting, advising guests of culinary proceedings throughout the dinner.

To conform to fashion's demand for volume and as wages were inexpensive but materials costly, the old slender silverware was tossed into the melting pot. It re-emerged with such weight, that anyone who brought food to his mouth felt the wealth of the host in his hand.

The array of cutlery, too, was boosted by having more components added to it. A small spoon with a cutting edge became essential for oyster eaters and lobster could not possibly be had without a tool devised specifically for that purpose. When cheese was sliced the knife conveniently could function as a fork as well.

Forks for escargots and knives for caviar, implements for fruit and others for butter. Ideas abounded and spread out primarily from the Anglo-Saxon world, such as fish cutlery.

Iron blades of knives left an aftertaste to fish and so two forks were used instead. Now these blades were substituted by silver, and with a corresponding fork, the new pair joined the already bulging set of silver.

Lavishly decorated food testifies not only to the taste of that time but also to the attitude towards wages in house and kitchen. Hours of fiddling work lay behind the presentation of a menu after which it was granted a minute or so for general admiration before the hostess, as the first, cut up the masterpiece.

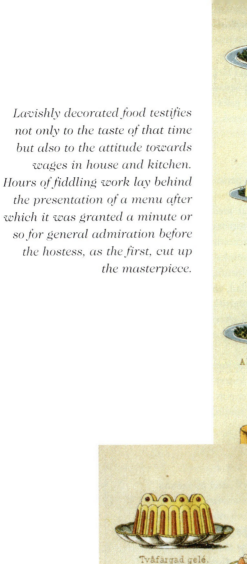

Stekt höna. Fasan.

Paj på vildt med gelé.

Små kräftpastejer. Ostronpastejer.

Hummer salad.

A la daube på hummer. A la daube på gris.

Paj på kapun.

Rysk salad.

arnerad tunga.

Tvåfärgad gelé. Vaniljpudding.

Macedoine af frukter och gelé.

Victoriasmörgåsar. Maränger.

Vindrufvegelé. Chokoladekräm.

Blanc-mangerpudding med frukt.

Apelsingelé. Vinpudding.

Kokta päron.

Glacebröd. Kanderad frukt.

Äpplepudding à la parisienne.

The Feminine Touch

Henriette Danneskiold-Samsøe was 47 years of age, a widow and the mother of seven when, in 1825, she opened the glass works of Holmegaard near the manor of that name. The idea was conceived by her newly deceased husband, but it was to be carried out by the industrious countess.

Since the loss of Norway, domestic glass manufacture no longer existed in Denmark except in Friederichsfeldt in the duchy of Slesvig. Here production had successfully been based on peat for fuel, and as Holmegaard included 1100 acres of peat bog the idea of likewise exploiting it was tempting.

To begin with it was a matter of meeting the demand for greenish glass such as bottles, windowpanes and retorts. An effort to acquire a monopoly for this type of merchandise was flatly refused by authorities. That did not stop the countess, however. She invited experts from abroad and then set to work. Already in 1826 sales amounted to 56.000 bottles, and in one decade this figure swelled to half a million.

Despite crises, fire and Norwegian as well as domestic competition Holmegaard retained its leading position. By the 1850's the assortment included a good number of other products, notably the clear drinking glass, that proved to be in great demand.

As the array of cutlery was growing, so did the variety of drinking glasses.

Glasses had moved from the sideboard to a fixed position in front of every seating. That required one for each of the numerous wines and with different shapes and heights.

Glass and silver weighed heavily on the middle class family struggling to keep up appearances. As for silver, plateware had become a remedy by the mid 18th century, and now glass was made affordable by an American invention of the 1830's.

Again mass production. Glass could now be manufactured by machine pressing. While its surface never obtained the same silky sheen as that of blown ones, it was perfectly suited for cutting.

Holmegaard produced its first pressed drinking glasses at the close of the century.

Ladies and Gentlemen

The original rigorous separation of sexes at dinners had gradually been modified in an effort to recognise the individuals´ rank and dignity. For such reasons place cards as a rule were shuffled differently as appears from the royal table plan of Christian VII´s birthday dinner in 1770. On less for-

mal occastions, however, one could take a seat as one pleased.

With the 19th century fashion prescribed, ladies and gentlemen alternated, in German called "bunte Reihe", which comes close to "mottled line". But in contrast to elsewhere, the Nordic countries placed the lady on

It was a major operation to manage a better-class dinner like this one just finished at the house of Brede. Had it not been for the staff hosts would be at a loss.

Upstairs and downstairs were two separated worlds – and yet – some dialogue is going on between the young gentleman on the right and the maid at the far left.

the gentleman's right, allegedly to enable him to attend his partner with his good hand.

The concept of pairing required an equal number of the two sexes, and given the prevailing deficiency of single men, widows and the unmarried were ignored and so slipped out of social life. As suggested by a commentator of the time, a ladies dinner now and then would suffice for their kind.

This was consistent with the slide that had occurred in woman's situation. Urbanisation and industrialism reduced her status to being based entirely upon that of her husband.

The attitude was primarily North-European, pronounced first of all in England, not surprisingly the hotbed of the suffragettes. The catholic "la mama" in contrast would hold on to her position, her husband dead or alive as might be.

Smoking was spreading and eventually included ladies as well. As addiction took hold it opened for ashtrays on the table. Later they were removed. But not among the Danes, they smoke as always.

Illumination

The extravagant burning of wax-candles as practised by the upper classes was reserved for festive occasions. In everyday life even courtiers had to grope their way through corridors by the flare of a single candlestick.

Then in the 1830´s the oil lamp found its way into the homes. A couple of decades later stearin composites were developed. In the beginning these were hardly less expensive than those of wax. Soon, however, the price fell and they filtered into broader parts of the population, casting brilliance upon special events.

In the 1860´s paraffin lamps followed suit. It became the popular common light source soon to be supplemented in urban areas by gaslight, but by the turn of the century electricity shot up front. Electric current neither smoked nor smelled, nothing had to be replaced or refilled except for an occasional light bulb, and then it could burn in a vertical as well as a horizontal position, and even upside down.

Entirely new lamps were created to put this wonder to full use although it took some time to divorce it from crystals, festoons and golden bronze. Wires were drawn hither and thither, existing chandeliers were subject to keen manipulation and the stucco angels of the Baroque had bulbs screwed into their mouths. Not even candelabra or candlesticks escaped their threads.

There was one drawback, though. The intolerable wire dangling over the table cloth. Here determined enthusiasts came to a quick decision. They cut a hole in the cloth, drilled down through the table, made their way through the carpet and inserted the plug in a switch sunk in the parquet flooring.

Flowers

When fresh flowers were finally granted admission to the table, they quickly became almost indispensable.

It was an unbreakable rule that centerpieces or flowers should never prevent the guests from seeing each other across the table; flowers should always be below or just above eye level.

The simplest way of ensuring this was to chop off the stalks and arrange the blossoms on the tablecloth in neat patterns or monograms. This was a trick the decorators of restaurants and similar establishments soon became masters at.

A shallow bowl filled with simple offerings from the garden or roadside was more elegant than scattered flowers, but for a truly dazzling array, a centrepiece with matching candelabras or candlesticks was unbeatable. They could be of porcelain, silver or gilded bronze and, along with the wherewithal to own them, great skill in the art of flower arranging was a necessity.

Behind the centrepiece and candelabra in neo-Rococo, a sideboard is seen. This piece of furniture became indispensable for storing silver and other items for the table when not in use.

Table Manners

Table manners have been the object of scrutiny in every age – and it makes their observance no easier that they differ greatly from country to country.

The most comprehensive set of statutes came from the regime of the English nanny. A finger and thumb thrust into the salt cellar was the path to grief. No, no, the thing to do was to take the salt spoon, build a genteel pyramid on the edge of the plate and use this handy depot to sprinkle on the food as required. In some countries, using the condiment was only permissible before tucking in, and never, after. The first tactic indicated a personal need, the second a criticism of the cuisine.

French children were badgered into placing their hands neatly on the table; English children into keeping them out of temptation's way under it. Another English eccentricity was that all food should be eaten from the convex surface of the tines – even troublesome peas, which inevitably rolled off at the slightest attempt to put food to mouth unless securely anchored in a bed of mashed potato. In some societies, cutting into a potato with a knife was unthinkable. And with certain delicacies, such as asparagus, the only tools permissible were the fingers, irrespective of how much sauce was involved. In the past, glasses were handed to guests, now they had to pick them up themselves. Stems attracted fingers almost whereas before, it might just as well have been the foot.

The real trial came with the pudding or dessert. And woe betide anyone who shoved a spoon into their mouth. The maximum permissible for that implement was to assist in loading a fork. And yet there it lay, right under the eyes of the guest, a shining social tiger trap waiting to be fallen into.

Admonishing the dear little ones began in the nursery, often illustrated on special plates with edifying words. Such educational efforts, however, did not always bring the intended results.

Das jugendlich Vergnügen

Was Hänschen nicht lernt, wird Hans nicht wissen.

Service No. 1

In his heyday, the father of Danish porcelain, Frantz Henrich Müller, had stressed the importance of manufacturing "such items as may be of use to every man."

He concentrated his efforts accordingly on the blue and white ware, suitable for under-glaze painting and therefore much cheaper to make than the multi-coloured wares. What is more, the cobalt needed for the vivid blue paint was readily available within the borders of the dual monarchy – in Norway.

The Blue Fluted, also known as mussel painted, was the factory's first dinner service to go into production. The taste of the market for the oriental was still evident in the patterns. The stylised plum foliage of the Blue Fluted is also oriental in its origin, though with certain modifications after a stay in Meissen before it acquired its Copenhagen identity.

The term 'mussel painted' is open to interpretation. It may refer to the Muslim merchants who played an important part in bringing the first supplies of porcelain to Europe. Though a more likely explanation lies in the grooved surface of the rim of the plates, resulting in a verbal description ending as an epithet.

This service was to become more of an epitome of Denmark than either Müller or any one else could have dreamed of. The Nordic purity of the deep blue in stark contrast to the white background is evident already in the factory's logo - the three wavy lines, symbolising the three sea straits of the country. The sea has printed its mark on this nation of sailors and seafarers through a thousand years, and the colour of the sea on the Blue Fluted won a place in the heart of the Danes from the very beginning.

An atmosphere of Nordic fin-de-siecle rests over this octagonal beach pavilion unaltered since it was built in 1882.

It was fitted out partly as a private health resort with copper tubs on the lower floor and as a venue for light meals on the upper. The furniture is simple and rustic. We are in the countryside.

The table is laid in accordance with time and setting but without allowing nostagia to get out of hand. The cloth is linen. The short decanters are taken from old English travelling cases. The glasses, however, are new. The porcelain is Blue Fluted.

It did indeed become an item 'of use to every man'. In town and country, among the high and the lowly. The older generation of today may turn up their noses at the pattern, associating it as they do with the unexciting diet of wartime, but a new generation has arrived and once again taken it to their hearts.

Müller's utility product has become a national heritage. Through 225 years of political and social change, new lifestyle and the fads of fashion, it has proved its stamina and vitality; and, indeed, with its success as an export product, carved out a place for itself in the part of the world it came from, the Far East.

The Blue Fluted is produced today just as it was in 1775 when the first service came out of the kilns. And every piece still bears, next to the artist's initials, the figure 1.

*The Blue Fluted used
for a simple lnch, 1884.
It adorned the
bourgeois dining room
of 1904 and is used by the
Royal Family as shown
here at Marselisborg Palace, 1996.*

Town and country

The increasing affluence of the 18th century had brought its benefits only as far as the towns and cities. In the country, famine was still the inevitable legacy of a crop failure and left little or no room for change in usages and customs.

But the new century brought reforms that created new landowners, influential farmers and well-heeled tenant farmers. They stood on the social ladder, peering up trying to gain a glimpse of how things were done among the squires.

Certain details they saw were easily copied, the tablecloth and fork, for example, and drinking habits such as quenching the thirst with copious amounts of warm beverages. Tea and coffee, in particular, oozed their way into everyday life and seeped down through the layer cake of society and gradually de-alcoholised a drunken peasantry.

A meal consumed in the home of the lowest peasant, however, remained much as it had been since the Renaissance. Grace said before a meal was as natural an event as it was in that era, and the men had their fixed places at the bench below the window.

The women sat on stools, closest to the kitchen, or ate standing, if they took part in the meal at all.

Cutlery was still individual property. If you were invited to share a meal, you took your knife with you; a spoon hewed out of wood or animal horn was placed conveniently on a nearby beam, and everybody ate from the same common bowl. At a farm with several workers, there was an unbreakable hierarchy as to who ate first – the foreman before his deputy, the cowhand before the day worker.

THE NORDIC TABLE

-What are they having now?
-Fish. Shall I lift youp?
-No, I'll wait for the meat.

The oilcloth became the answer for many small families. All it needed was a quick wipe and, if necessary, a slap with the paintbrush to brighten it up a bit. But even the humblest of farmhouses would have a cloth hidden away, ready to be produced if the vicar should drop by. Not that the family got much enjoyment from this costly item - it covered only that part of the table immediately in front of the guest. Because according to ancient tradition, although social unequals might share a meal at the same table, they might never share the same cloth.

Housekeeping in the country was a question of self-sufficiency and demanded the sweat of many brows. But even in the towns, with their range of shops and markets, cooking was a time-consuming and troublesome issue. Bachelors with no domestic servants could not just pop a steak on a hot plate or beat an omelette for themselves. They had to rely on family, friends or public eating places, which advertised their services by hanging signs in front of their establishments. One of these displays from 1821 proclaims the virtues of N.F. Wilsted's eating house in the old centre of Copenhagen, offering hot meals 'morning, noon and evening.'

The abject poverty of the country spread to the towns. Burgeoning industry left an ever-growing swathe of social losers behind it – sick factory workers and their children, the dregs of society or those of unfortunate birth.

S. Kröyer pinx — Skagen 1883

ANCHER   V. PETERS

DTF. PETERSEN   CHR. LUNDH   BRØNDUM   KROUTHÉN   O. BJØRG   KROHG

The Age of Beauty

In the foreground the Norwegians Christian Krogh and Charles Lundh. Then clockwise their compatriots Eilif Petersen and Wilhelm Peters, the hotel keeper Degn Brøndum, the Swedes Johan Krouthén and Oscar Björck. In the background Michael Ancher is leaving to go shooting.

The Victorian style stood its ground for the rest of the century and longer, although with inevitable evolution. New trends were making themselves felt.

"Endlessly eating, drinking, discussing" – the image of the painters from all the Nordic countries who gathered at Skagen, at the northern tip of Denmark, as the century drew to a close. Brøndum's Hotel was the recurring rendezvous and their table reflected their style of living.

The choice of colours was ripe for a change and soon white became right. Light was beckoned inside, flickering through the gossamer lace of the summer curtains. And white shimmered in the flimsy folds of women's gowns.

A generation earlier it would have been unthinkable for a lady to reveal as much as the tips of her toes from under the cupola of her crinoline, and many small boys were under the impression that the fairer sex was fitted with some sort of wheeled trolley affair instead of legs.

But skirts lost their girth and were given a lift that was to be the first of many on the long road ahead.

The age had a glow of carefree optimism. Every invention, it was thought, had already been made – the telephone, electricity, the film, the motor car and even the flying machine. The imagination could stretch no further. The skies were blue and God was in his heaven. It was La Belle Époque

The sun shines unhindered on the fan palm. Women did not have the right to vote, of course, and when the first few of their number took a higher education many found it a little strange. But they did read - even newspapers of the more controversial kind.

THE NORDIC TABLE

Neo-Classicism

The imitation of classic style is obvious in flower vases and basins festooned with drapes of vertical lines.

Classicism came back into fashion. The attempt to resuscitate its symmetry and clean lines was evident in such items as the ornate table decoration known as the jardinière, complete with fountains, statuettes, vases and the pillars of the classical age. They were made in faience, porcelain or, for the real aficionado, in glass.

Short, stubby columns form the outer rim of this mirror-glass plateau, complete with a baroque garden and fountains, all in Venetian glass.

Art Nouveau

In Belgium, and before long France, a brand new style arrived, partly as a protest to Neo-Classicism – Art Nouveau.

Its exuberant sweeping lines derived particular inspiration from plants and Japanese art. It wound its joyous way into the wonderful universe of frivolity. The pallette verged on the brown, but also embraced the green of decadence and satanic black. Its influence was seen not only in works of art but also in jewellery, dinner services, glass and cutlery.

As Art Nouveau spread to other countries, it acquired different personalities and different names.

The Germans produced a heavier version called Jugend, which in turn sired the Danish style, Skønvirke.

Chandeliers 1920

Master of Silver

It is said of Georg Jensen that he never followed fashion, he created it. He himself did not put it quite like that. There was a poster hanging in his workshop declaring: "Never follow the stream, follow the times if you want to keep your youth and vitality in the struggle."

Georg Jensen was both a silversmith and sculptor. He opened his first small workshop with a single apprentice in Copenhagen in 1904. He made jewellery and belt buckles in amber and semi-precious stone, much influenced by the world of botany. But as more and more customers beat a path to his door, the company started accepting commissions for large pieces of hollowware in silver.

The style is Georg Jensen's own refinement of the dominating Jugendstil; it is voluptuous and sculptural, almost monumental. A hallmark of his work is his use of patination. It imparts a dull, almost steel-like sheen to the precious metal, approaching the black of night at the bottom of a hammering.

His works awoke delight and enthusiasm from the very beginning and in just over thirty years, the little workshop grew to a global business with hundreds of employees. Equally important is the fact that it created a fertile seedbed for new talent, essential for the survival of the company when the master was no longer around.

Georg Jensen worked before, during and after the Great War that tore the old way of life up by the roots. He created fashion, he foresaw changes of taste and style and his works belong to tomorrow as much as yesterday.

On his death in 1935, the New York Herald Tribune wrote in his obituary "the greatest silversmith in three centuries."

Georg Jensen standing behind one of his apprentices in the workshop 1908.

Fruit basket 1919

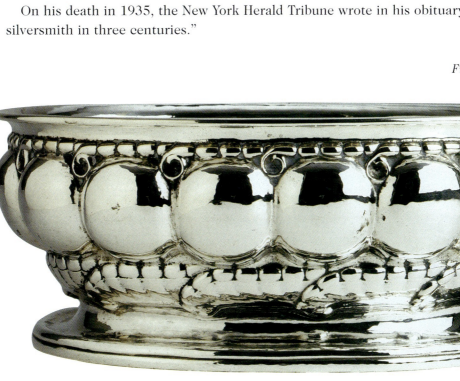

"*Whereas in England the host and hostess sit at the end of the table, in France they face each other across the middle, the ends being reserved for low people, those who have married for love and so on.*

Two years of love, we say here, are no compensation for a lifetime at the end of the table."

Nancy Mitford

The poor relative

Danish faience

Danish faience was born at the factory on Store Kongensgade in Copenhagen in the 1720s. Royal concession was granted to Holstein-born Johan Wolff but limited him to the production of blue and white ware.

Wolff's behaviour was true to form of many of the pioneers of porcelain. He managed to steal some of the expensive cobalt and most of the key people at the factory before absconding to a managerial position at the newly founded Swedish company Rörstrand.

But Store Kongensgade continued, albeit under difficult conditions. Bickering among the managers and competition from the new Danish factories like Kastrup and Blaataarn ended in a legal battle. Store Kongensgade was forced to close down in 1769.

The factory had produced not only daily consumer goods, serving dishes, plates and flower vases; it also created weightier items such as tray tables that set a trend that raged throughout the Nordic countries.

Bowl with lid decorated in blue from Store Kongensgade. It is badly chipped but nevertheless a museum piece.

Multicoloured bowl with lid from Kastrup.

Kastrup was granted its royal concession in 1755, with considerable interest from the palace. It approved the production of all wares except the blue and white ware for which Store Kongensgade still had the monopoly at that time. Instead, Kastrup became synonymous with multicoloured faience, possibly the finest in Denmark.

More factories were opended, all using traditional methods. The fired clay was covered with a white glaze that created the base colour, then painted and fired again.

But in the course of the 18th century, the British had developed a new technique. They processed the clay so that it became white in itself and then applied a transparent lead glaze over the decorations. This technique increased the durability and lowered the price.

The Danish companies were protected by an effective barrier of import duties until 1797. Then, one by one, they had to close.

The Duchies

The faience of the Crown Duchies of Slesvig and Holstein was noted for its colourful decorations, with inspiration coming from France, particularly from Strasbourg.

Vivid colours, apart from blue, were sensitive to high temperatures. Pieces were protected by putting them into the kiln in a sort of capsule, a technique known as muffle firing.

The factory in Kiel started operation in 1763, with the former Meissen worker Tönnich among its employees. When it finally shut down in 1787, Kiel had produced bowls, serving dishes, plates and inkwells for everyday use, but also in the product basket were costly objects such as tray tables and stove superstructures.

Kellinghusen was no fewer than six independent factories, all located in Holstein in a small town of the same name. The location was suitable because of its deposits of clay and a river that facilitated transport of the finished wares. The first of these factories was granted a royal concession in 1765, the last shut down in 1865.

The later period is particularly known for its lighter wares, intended for the kitchen and servants' hall. Although they were treated accordingly – even the dogs ate off them – enough has survived to whet the appetite of collectors.

Kiel Faience c. 1770 with dishes, centrepiece and a tureen.

Table laid with Kellinghusen dishes c. 1840. The yellow rim is typical of the period. The mug has a tin lid, not shown.

Marieberg

When former court dentist Johan Ludvig Eberhard Ehrenreich, the founder of Marieberg, abandoned his dream of making porcelain, he shifted his attention to faience, specialising in the glazed creamware intended for everyday use.

More exclusive pieces were also manufactured, with motifs of flowers and birds in brilliant colours. Both aesthetically and technically, they matched the standards of the best manufacturers in Europe. Later, vases, glazed tiles for stove decoration and tray tables were also produced, though in limited numbers.

The economy, however, was failing and in 1782, the factory was sold, only to be closed six years later.

At this time, Ehrenreich had long since left Sweden, more than likely a bitter man. His lifelong ambition was never fulfilled, but his reputation enjoys the greatest respect among connoisseurs of Swedish faience.

Enameled potpourri vase from Marieberg.

Still life with a cream coloured Marieberg tureen of the kind which unfortunately seldom lasted long.

Punch, popes
and Bishop's Bowls

In the early 18th century, punch became fashionable. It was a drink that came from England and consisted mostly of red wine mixed with sugar and exotic fruits.

In Copenhagen at that time, there was a group of gentlemen who called themselves the Pope Society. The rank and dignity of the pope was, of course, attributed to its chairman, whilst the rank and file members bore titles such as cardinals, bishops and their subordinates.

One of them was a man by the name of Rasmus Ærebo. He was manager of the Store

Kongensgade factory, which explains why the factory produced a special version of a punch bowl called the Bishop's Bowl.

Others, too, gathered round the punch bowl, among them the Swedish artists Sergel and Ehrensvärd, Baron de Geer and the Danish painter Abildgaard.

In 1796-97, they visited each other frequently, hotly debating morals, politics and, of course women, particularly the worst of the kind - the powerful and unfaithful.

One of their number was the Baron's wife, Aurora, portrayed in Chinese company on page 49. And, of course, they discussed the merits of punch.

The subjects of their discourses were expressed in words and a wealth of pictures they sent to each other.

Around the table sit Pope, cardinals and bishops. The Bishop's bowl appeared with different decorations, here with the confident motto: "King and country are faring well."

Abildgaard at his desk, while Jomfru Møller, the housekeeper leans against the bowl to watch de Geer and Sergel bathing in the punch.

The Baron drowning in punch.

*The setting is Italian but the artist, Slott-Møller, is a Dane and his choise of faience
hardly accidental. For a few years Slott-Møller was employed by Aluminia.*

THE NORDIC TABLE

Aluminia

Danish faience underwent a renaissance in 1862. The factory was given the name, Aluminia, and it had learned from English expertise.

Faience became more and more fashionable and was no longer banished to the kitchen. Country life was enjoying increasing popularity – with it came a growing demand for tableware at a more reasonable price. And many began to fall for the special charm of faience.

Fans of faience rather than porcelain often compare their differences to wood and steel. The first is 'organic, warm and alive', the latter 'cold and lifeless'. The explanation for faience's special qualities lies in the lower firing temperatures, which allow a wider choice of colours and thereby an entirely different depth and intensity.

As a small sample of his line the original drawing for a marmelade jar.

*Christian Joachim´s self-portrait
on a faience plate.*

*Blue Pheasant tableware in its present
version presented in a modern framework
with lemons to balance the
colour-saturated plates.
Like many modern tables this one is not
really wide enough for decorations in the
middle. So as not to get squeezed it has
been arranged across the near the end.*

The father of the new faience was
Christian Joachim of Aluminia. The style
was his own and it achieved international
acclaim, winning the Grand Prix at the
World Exhibition in St. Louis in 1904.

Today, works from his time are
collectors items. A few are still in production and a few others have been
resurrected, although in a different form –
the Blue Pheasant, for a example.

*The original Blue Pheasant
as presented on a vase.*

Although there were strong trade links with the Far East, none of the Nordic countries became colonial powers of any significance.

Denmark, for instance, had but a few trading stations on that long trade route. And it could take several months before her sailors saw their own colours flying in the shimmering tropical heat above some remote coastline. One of these stations or mini-colonies was Tranquebar, on the Madras coast of India.

When Aluminia launched a new faience service in 1914 and named it Traquebar, the colony had long been out of Danish hands. Yet the name is very fitting. The central motif of a blue tulip could hardly be more European. But the body of the faience is vaguely grey and the glaze with a hint of bluish green, a combination of colours that nicely complements the china porcelain.

This unusual table decoration belongs to a Danish family, which, after some years in Shanghai, brought home a considerable oriental collection, mainly Chinese porcelain.
 In the centre, an incense dome, surrounded by twelve fable figurines. Each has its own animal head, symbolising the twelve names of the Chinese years.

"If only the soup had been as hot as the wine,
the wine as old as the fish,
the fish as young as the maid,
and the maid as willing as the hostess,
then it would have been a most charming evening."

Anonimous

Out in the open

Summer is coming

Ants in the grass, flies on the food and wasps settling on anything sweet. Despite all these adversities, people have always delighted in taking a meal outdoors.

The Scandinavians of long ago willingly braved the risk of cold feet and an aching back, because the arrival of summer also meant the arrival of light.

When the grey-black pencil lines of the forest burst into effervescent green and the sun rose a few hours after midnight, the gentlefolk moved outdoors with food, wine and a pack of cards.

French wines, with the exception of claret, were not all that fashionable during the Nordic renaissance. Rhine wine were perferred and it was the custom then to add one's own mix of spices and sweeten it with a congenial blend of honey and sugar.

Johan Friis had Hesselager built for him at the island of Funen. Completed in 1550 the manor at its second storey displays a contemporary fresco depicting the family spending a day in the open. Bread and large drinking goblets are seen. A flautist and drummer provide the music, pitchers are kept cool, and the dog has acquired his share.

Rococo, dignity and orderly manners. Fresh air is enjoyable but must certainly be moderated. Here the ducal family of Slesvig-Holsten on the terrace.

Since heathen days shepherds have welcomed the onset of summer with festivities. But outdoor life was a pleasure for the wealthy.

The house in the background is not a modest one, and the cloth is covered with tin plates and even a fine little show-dish in the form of a paté of pheasant. Bread, wine and pitchers, lute playing and animated flirtation.

People of the Renaissance, devout as they were, prayed intensely as seen in paintings and tomb stones. But not every hour of the day was spent on thoughts of the hereafter. Mundane life had its needs too and time was found for various other pursuits.

143

After 1900, many townspeople of limited means sought the pleasures of country life by spending the summer on a farm, revelling in the livestock and lush, green meadows.

Farmers normally welcomed these guests and their romantic notions but after a hard day in the fields in fickle weather, they failed to see the charm of nature.

Sound bourgeois economy is visible in these two table arrangements
with their tea urns. Normally they were a small pot with strong tea and
a large kettle with boiling water.
Left, the artist has preferred a southern setting – right, breakfast
is ready in a Swedish garden.

THE NORDIC TABLE

The Skagen colony of artists, too, moved into the open. From left
sitting: Martha Johansen. Standing: Viggo Johansen, P.S Krøyer,
Degn Brøndum, Michael Ancher, Thorvald Niss, Oscar Björk;
then Helene Christensen and Anna Ancher with her daughter,Helga.

The wine is sparkling and glasses are held as prescribed at the time.
The menu is unknown, but Viggo Johansen´s birthday present to his
hostess, Anna Ancher, in 1887, suggests she was fond of sea food.

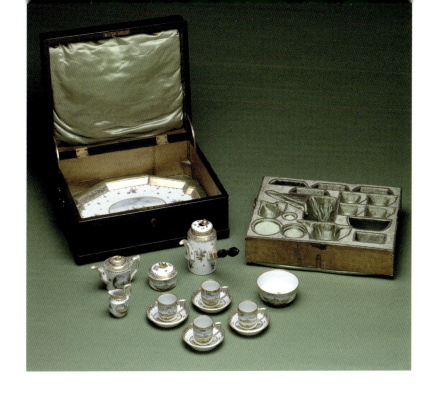

All transportation of goods was a problematic, and sometimes risky, business – especially by land, on roads that could be measured in length, breadth and as well as in depth.

Careful packing, therefore, was a vital necessity. If the fragile and precious porcelain was to survive a long journey to a buyer, or even an afternoon's outing to the countryside, it had to be lovingly protected.

This veneered wooden case has a lining of green sateen, and every cup and jug rest safely in its own individually fashioned cavity.

The set from The Royal Copenhagen Porcelain dated 1787. The small pot is for tea, the large one for chocolate. The latter has an opening in the lid for a whisk to prevent skin forming and the chocolate settling.
An economic health-cookbook of 1800 – they were on the shelves even then - is highly critical of this habit:: "Foam remains foam. It is superfluous gas thereby entering the stomach and needlessly causing wind."

When, a hundred years later, parties went on the hunt, portable boxes were more simple but drinking so much more elaborate. Thirst was quenched with champagne.

Danish officers were being well looked after during a break in a military manoeuvre in 1886.

Just over twenty years earlier, Denmark had lost the Duchies of Slesvig and Holstein to Prussia. At this stroke, Denmark, the once most powerful factor in the north, had withered to the point were its ability so survive as a sovereign nation was in doubt.

Perhaps as a natural consequence, there was a need to reassure the people of the existence of the many regiments by public displays of their uniforms.

From right, a captain of the Royal Guard, a captain of horse from the dragoons, a captain of the Infantry, a captain of the Artillery and, standing with raised cigar, a captain of the Engineers. To the left a horse-guardsman salutes his general.

Consistent with their rank, the table is laid white cloth, claret is brougt in a crate along with beer and aquavit. Judging by the bottles in the foreground somebody has possibly broken away for a premature start. The private soldiers in the background do not seem to have gone short either - only the style is different.

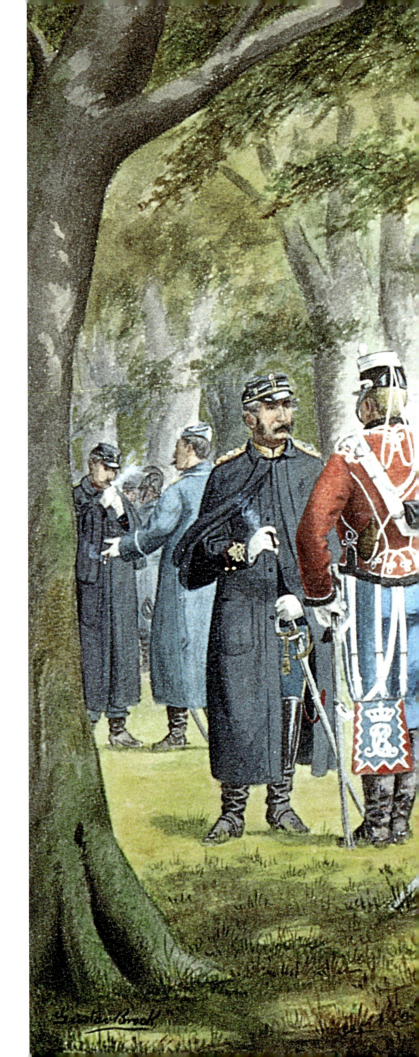

Crayfish became a popular delicacy throughout Sweden in the late 19th century. Until then, it was seen only on the tables of the court and nobility. Carl von Linné regarded them as unfit for human consumption, whereas the great Swedish poet Bellmann described how they "shine scarlet in the cooking pot". Because if you had to eat them, you had to eat them hot.

But the annual crayfish orgy only became a national instiution when so many of the small crustaceans were being devoured that the government introduced a quota system.

From that day on, the opening of the crayfish season has been celebrated with a feast, a peculiarly Swedish ritual of songs and snaps, one tot per crayfish tail.

Catching them yourself is always exciting and here the whole family is involved.

Even under the most countryfied conditions the women and little girlsa kept their hats on to prevent their skin being tanned by the sun.Only the girl in the lake, in deep concentration, has shoved hers back off her head.

In the foreground the table stands ready for the great event. White cloth, tin plates and jugs and of course the decanter with the indispensable aquavit..

THE NORDIC TABLE

The table of lackered iron is laid with greenery amidst greenery.
Dock leaves serve as table mats, and as beds for silver dishes
an adventurous but succesful combination. Vines of ivy and
angelica have transformed the shaft of the parasol into a may pole.

The Nordic people adore grilling. The barbecue had a break-though with
the charter tourism in post war years. It revives happy memories of warm
evenings spent under the palm trees of the Mediterranian.
*   The grill itself may be nothing more than a discarded box from*
a supermarket or a collapsible ligthweight framework or - as shown
here – a table custom-built for the purpose.

"*If nature had been comfortable, mankind would never have invented architecture.*"

Oscar Wilde.

New Patterns

THE NORDIC TABLE

The kitchen-diner

A country kitchen with old style cupboards and comfortable space between eating and working area.

Slabs of plaited bast serve as presentation plates.

First the staff of servants disappeared, then the last few maids and dining moved back to where it came from.

After almost five hundred years of segregation, oven and stove, pots and pans were once again the daily spectators of the consumption of the meal they had produced. Food was eaten where it was prepared - in the kitchen. The most neglected room in the house became the most important and assumed as much status as the motor car.

A completely new industry emerged. Architects and designers created sophisticated holistic solutions that matched the new era's alliance of advanced machinery, great affluence and, the most precious commodity of all, time.

The small city kitchen was put to optimal use with room for four. Blue check pattern cloth and charming fish plates set the tone.

Family focal point

From early morning to early evening the family was scattered around crèche, kindergarten, school, youth club and office. Shopping was a hectic, hasty affair undertaken on the way home.

The kitchen became the focal point of the family, the venue for what became known as 'quality time' and family activities. Cooking and eating, homework and tele-vision, catching up with each other's daily lives, cosy chat and creative pursuits – even guitar playing.

The room is arranged around an old chimney, now accomodating fire place and ventilation combined. It also separates table from cooking area. The architect was called upon to make the working table sturdy enough to carry half an ox. We are not told if it has been put to such a test.

Simplification

Books on how to behave at table and how to lay it have been written for centuries. And manuals will doubtless continue to appear for those who want to be shepherded through the pitfalls and fog banks of social niceties. For what was a serious matter yesterday might easily be a laughing matter tomorrow.

Shortage of time has sharpened our focus on the practical. The family silver has given way to stainless steel – who has the time or inclination to polish it? The credibility of the decanter took a body blow during the Second World War when the most doubtful fluids were poured from otherwise honourable crystal. Since then, the bottle has been accepted at table, with a label that vouches for its pedigree, humble or grand.

And again we return to the old chestnut of the correct way to hold a glass. First it was nearly always by the foot. Gradually the fingers crept upwards and took an indelicate grasp of the stem – but never further. Touching the cup of the glass was taboo, as it was generally accepted that the temperature of the wine would suffer as a result. Perhaps some inquisitive soul has put this theory to the test or perhaps the grip proved too awkward to survive. For whatever reason, most people now conjoin aesthetics with practicality by holding the cup.

Once upon a time, a short prayer of thanksgiving was said before every meal – grace. Since then, veneration of the maker has given way to a respect for home economics. Food must not be wasted – what was taken should be eaten. But the ethical issue of leftovers has now faded almost to insignificance.

It began decades ago when restaurant owners heavy-handedly deposited portions of food before the defenceless guest. Then came the practice of arranging a dish artistically on the plates before serving – blessed with five strokes of the fork through the puddle of tomato sauce and adorned with a flimsy sculpture of lemon balm. But for the older generation, it is still a horrifying thought that the rubbish bin is the final victor of culinary combat.

Certain Nordic customs appear to be invincible. Glasses are clinked together when the traditional skål is given and the Danish hostess is showered with compliments after the meal, even if the sauce turns out to be burned and the roast dry as dust. And the lady is still seated on the right of the gentleman, despite the confusion this can create in an international gathering.

Rules of suitable conduct for host and guest are endless and extremely diverse. Some of them are founded on common sense; others are relics from a dim and distant past; and others still have no other intention than to put up territorial boundaries.

The cold table

For centuries it has been a practice to cover a piece of rye bread with dripping. When placing a piece of meat or fish on top of it – the open sandwich was born.

The Scandinavian cold table was a refinement of that invention and won great favour towards the end of the 19th century. It was a cuisine ideally suited for the lunch table and the retail trade lost no time in developing new specialities, with modest households as their core customers; grander homes made their own.

The wider the repertoire, the more elaborate became their garnishing. In 1939, the Danish cooking celebrity Ingeborg Suhr decreed that the table should appear 'tasteful' and display 'a well-bred sense of colour.'

Such a declaration gave carte blanche for decorating dishes with roses, lilies and daisies carved from carrot, raddish or turnip and secured to the food with toothpicks. Shredded leaks made beautiful chrysanthemums and swedes exquisite swans.

Today, the cold table is known to all, even if its popularity is dwindling. Few people eat lunch at home and restaurants nowadays offer buffets or plates of the day. And Miss Suhr's contribution has been put on the shelf.

When it is done, the Scandinavian cold table is considerably simpler, although the ingredients are much the same. Starting with herring in sundry variations, it continues through patés and several kinds of meats to the cheese. Each guest is free to devise his own menu to suit his taste and pallet. Though the comparison should not be taken too far, it is a meal similar in principle to the grand 'service à la Française'.

A lighter version of the. cold table. In the middle, a composite dish for various treats. Table ware is Royal Copenhagen called "Tureby".

Arne Jacobsen

Arne Jacobsen (1902-71) made his breakthrough as an architect around 1930, when he introduced functionalism in Denmark in a number of building projects. After the war, his work expanded to embrace design in its broadest sense. Some of it can be seen in the Royal Hotel in Copenhagen, built 1958-60. He not only designed the building but also its lamps, fittings, door handles, clocks, textiles and furniture, including the famous Swan and Egg chairs. Even glass and cutlery were created on his drawing board.

His style of design soon won world fame. And much of the inventory that can still be seen at the hotel was put into series production.

In restaurant "Alberto K" At the top of the Royal Hotel, guests overlook the city and the Tivoli Garden while taking their meal in surroundings created in every detail by the great architect.

As you like it

In the post-war years, supermarkets displayed groceries as pre-packed items, replacing the casks and churns used for commodities such as butter.

Their arrival heralded the end of an era – the days of buying by the ounce were numbered and cartons of milk, yoghurt and squeeze bottles invaded the table.

But there were still occasions when a well-laid table was nevertheless desirable, even necessary - the boss coming to dinner, a family milepost or just a meal out of the ordinary.

With the demise of the parlour maid and the obligatory damask tablecloth, came the opportunity for creativity and free expression. Conformity made way for individuality. It was not the purse that set the limit but the imagination. Tables were gay or simple, bright or sombre, monochrome or or technicoloured. They were laid with extravagance or economy, on tablecloths, plastic, wood, glass or metal. In every material and every colour. Nothing was taboo.

Scrolls and gild disappeared when modern design took over illumination.

Steel, glass, plastic, coarse napkins and a virtual ban on colours as decreed by the naked look of minimalism.

*New wrought iron combined with old prisms,
but it needs a high ceiling.*

*The green of stems strikingly contrasts
the red of the table cloth. These kitchen
facilities were completed in 1988.
Iron stove, black tiles and copper utentils
are reminiscent of ancestral hearths.*

The landscapes of Denmark are surrounded by the sea. The people feel drawn by the water, to sail on, swim in or just gaze at.

A family of the present age was about to build a manor house. It was some distance from the coast but there was a small lake on the property. As plans proceeded, the idea of building a dining room as an extension to the house on piles driven into the lake became more and more appealing. It was fitted with french windows opening onto a small footbridge.

Simple, delicate and romatic. A sturdy natural-coloured linen cloth with a heavy seam hits the tile floor and is broken by a small white upper cloth. The combined choise of colours is continued in plate and napkin.

Long- stemmed glasses find their element in these peaceful surroundings. The seasons' flowers are arranged in an ice bowl. Candlesticks can be recognised from page 116.

The table is zinc, the candlesticks black iron. The picture shows a little steel, a little tin, old glasses and green- yellow flowers. The tableware is Royal Copenhagen´s most recent arrival, Liselund.

The first sea-tureen from 1976 by Arne Griegst.

Arje Griegst was trained as a goldsmith and created some extraordinary pieces of jewellery. In 1978, he also designed one of the most unusual dinner services of our time, Triton, living proof that Scandinavian design does not necessarily mean simple lines. The same applies to a series of drinking glasses he made for Holmegaard in 1983.

The sea and its creatures were a strong inspiration and his first soup tureen is like something born of the foam of a breaking wave.

His work completes the circle, a restatement of the ties to a distant past; to the days when the early China-farers made their arduous treks through desert and over mountain to the Middle Empire. There they met the new and the wonderful, this fine, white ware named porcelain after the shell of the sea snail Porcella.

When asked by the press how a glass should be held:
"It doesn't matter, as long as you drink from it."

HRH Prince Henrik of Denmark, August 2000.

Illustrations

Front page: Beach pavillon.
Foto: Bjørn Wennerwald.

p. 2-3. Table with faience.
Photo: Jesper Weng.

p. 9. The Last Supper.
(detail) Jerg Ratgeb,
c. 1500. Museum
Boijmans van Beuningen,
Rotterdam. Photo: Bridgeman
Art Library/ Bodil Bjerring.

p. 10. The Last Supper,
15th. century. The Church
of Gerlev, Denmark.
Photo: National Museet
København.

p. 12. Silkcloth, (detail)
1621. The Kremlin.
Photo: Kunstindustrimuseet,
København / Anita Schulin.

p. 13. Still. Willem Claesz,
1648. Hermitage, St. Petersburg.
Photo: Bridgeman Art Library /
Bodil Bjerring.

p. 14-15. The Ulfeldt family,
artist unknown, 1621.
Frederiksborgmuseet.
Photo: Hans Petersen.

p. 16. The Rich Man´s Table,
(detail). Karmelitterklostret,
Helsingør. Photo: E.S.

p. 17. Cutlery of gold and
agate. First half of the 17th
century. Rosenborg.
Photo: W.A.

p. 18. Kermesse, (detail)
Pieter Breughel, 1568.
Kunsthistorisches Museum,
Wien. Photo: Bridgeman
Art Library / Bodil Bjerring.

p. 19. The King Drinks, (detail),
Jacob Jordaens, c. 1650, Kunst-
historisches Museum, Wien.
Photo: Bodil Bjerring.

p. 20. Silkcloth, 1621.
The Kremlin.
Photo: Kunstindustrimuseet,
København / Anita Schulin.

p. 21. Gilded silver ship,
Amsterdam 1595-96. Hermitage,
St. Petersburg. Photo: Bridgeman
Art Library / Bodil Bjerring.

p.22. Still with peacock
pate, (detail) Pieter Claesz 1627.
Photo: The Bridgeman Art
Library / Bodil Bjerring.

p. 23. The Temptation of
St. Anthony, (detail).
Hieronimus Breughel,
c. 1500. Museo Nacionale
de Arte Antiga, Lisboa.
Photo: Bridgeman Art Library /
Bodil Bjerring.

p. 24-25. Painting by Henrik
Gyldenstierne, 1613.
Håndskriftsamlingen.
Det Kgl. Bibliotek. København.

p. 26. Goblet, Kungsholm,
c.1690. Nationalmuseum
Stockholm. Photo: Nationalmuseum,
Stockholm.

p. 27. Pasglass. 17th century.
Rosenholm. Photo Sys Ehlers.

p. 27. Rosenholm Castle.
Photo: Sys Ehlers.

p. 28-29. Peasant Wedding, Pieter
Breughel, 1568. Kunsthistorische
Museum, Wien. Photo: Bridgeman
Art Libraby / Bodil Bjerring.

p. 30. Scanian Inn, (detail).
Govert Camphuysen,
1650. Malmø Museum.
Photo: Bodil Bjerring.

p. 59. J.F. Struensee, Christian August Lorentzen. Det National-historiske Museum på Frederiks-borg. Photo: Hans Petersen.

p. 59. Queen Caroline Mathilde, Francis Cotes 1766. Det National-historiske Museum på Frederiks-borg. Photo: Frederiksborgmuseet / Hans Petersen.

p. 59. Mustard Jars, Jørgen Nielsen Gram, mid 18th century. Det Kgl. Sølvkammer, København. Photo: Lennart Larsen.

p. 60. Tureen on plateau, Niels Gram, mid 18th century. Det Kgl. Sølvkammer, København. Photo: Lennart Larsen.

p. 61. Masquarade (detail), Benoit le Coffre 1711. Frederiksberg Slot. Photo: Bodil Hallstrøm.

p. 62. New Year at Stockholm Palace 1779, Pehr Hilleström 1779. Nationalmuseum, Stock-holm. Photo: Bridgeman Art Libra-ry / Bodil Bjerring.

p. 63. Tureen of gold and silver, Robert Joseph Auguste 1775-76. H. M. Kongen af Sveriges samlin-ger, Sverige. Photo: Magnus Pers-son / Bodil Bjerring.

p. 64. The Hermitage north of Copenhagen, J.J. Bruun, 1741. Rosenborg, København. Photo: Kit Weiss.

p. 65. Hermitage at Fredensborg castle. A.E.Willarst. 1727. Rosenborg, København. Photo: Kit Weiss

p. 66-67. Lunch with Oysters, Jean-Francois de Troy. 1735. Chantilly, Musée Condé. Photo: Bridgeman Art Library / Bodil Bjerring.

p. 68-69. Flora Danica tureen. Royal Copenhagen. Photo: Jesper Weng.

p. 70. Gripsholm tureen, 1775. Kungl. Husgerådskammaran, Stockholm. Photo: Alexis Daflos.

p. 71. The Gribsholm Service.1775. Ôstasiatiska Museet, Stockholm. Photo: Erik Cornelius.

p. 72. Queen Jualiane Marie. Virgilius Eriksen, 1778. Statens Museum for Kunst, København. Photo: Hans Petersen.

p. 73. The factory i Købmagergade. 1872. Royal Copenhagen.

p. 74. Carl von Linné. Schäffer, 1739. Hammerby Museet. Uppsala.

p. 75. Semper Augustus. Judith Leyster, 1643. Frans Hals Museum, Halem. Photo: Bodil Bjerring.

p. 76-77. Linnaea Borealis. Royal Copenhagen.

p. 76-77. Flora Danica plate. Det kgl. Sølvkammer, København. Photo: Lennart Larsen.

p. 78. H.M. The Queen´s cover, 1990. Det Kgl. Sølvkammer, København. Photo: Lennart Larsen.

p. 79. Porcelain centrepiece, Flora Danica. Det Kgl. Sølvkammer, København. Photo: Lennart Larsen.

p. 80. The Church of Our Lady burning, seen from Landemærket. Lahde. Københavns Bymuseum. Photo: Hans Juhl.

p. 80. Queen Alexandra (detail). Edward Hughes, 1904. Det Nationalhistoriske Museum på Frederiksborg. Photo: Frederiksborgmuseet / Ole Haupt.

p. 81. The Battle of Copenhagen. Punchbowl, Royal Copenhagen. Det Nationalhistoriske Museum på Frederiksborg. Photo: Frederiks-borgmuseet / Ole Haupt.

p. 82-83. Modern Flora Danica, Royal Copenhagen. Photo: Jesper Weng.

p. 84. Flowers and butterflies by a ruin. Elias van den Broeck. With kind permission from Sotherby´s, London.

Bibliography

Andersen, Ellen: Bordskik, København 1971.

Antonsen, Inge Mejer: Omkring en chokoladekande, article i Budstikken 1960.

Becker, John: Damask og drejl – dækketøjets historie i Danmark, København 1989.

Benchard, Mogens: Notes on the Table in late 17th and early 18th Century Denmark, artikel i Rosenborg Studier, København 2000.

Benchard, Mogens m.fl.: Dansk Porcelæn 1775-2000 – design i 225 år, København 2000.

Blunt, Wilfred: Carl von Linné, London 1971.

Boyhus, Else-Marie: Historisk Kogebog – Komfuralderen, Århus 1978.

Braudel, Fernand: Structures of Everyday Life – The Limits of the Possible, vol 1., London 1981.

Danielsson, v. Märta-Stina: Svenskt Glas, Stockholm 1995.

Das Flora Danica Service 1790-1802, Den Kongelige Udstillingsfond, København 1999.

En Konges Taffel – guldsmedekunst og borddækning i det 18. århundrede, Statsinventarie-Kommisionen, København 1988.

Gad, Emma: Takt og Tone, København 1985.

Grandjean, Bredo: Flora Danica-stellet, København 1973.

Hernmarck, Carl: Fajans og Porslin, Stockholm 1959.

Holland, Margaret: Illustrated guide to silver, London 1985.

Hrasky, Øyunn Bjaaknæs: Nøstetangen Glass. Article i Interiør Magasinet, Oslo 1990.

Jexlev, Thelma, Peter Riismøller & Mogens Schlütter: Dansk glas i renæssancetid 1550-1650, 1970.

Johan Friederich Böttger zum Ehren, Leipzig 1982.

Kogebøger indeholdende 100 forstücker 1616, Århus 1966.

Lassen, Erik: Ske, kniv og gaffel, København 1960.

Lund, Troels: Dagligt Liv i Norden, 6. udgave, København 1968.

Marquardt, Klaus: Eight Centuries of European Knives, Forks and Spoons, Stuttgart 1997.

Mikkelsen, Leif Bering: Aluminia Fajance, København 2000.

Molesworth, Robert: En beskrivelse af Danmark, som det var i 1692, Wormianum 1978.

Ogier, Charles: Det store bilager i København 1634, København 1964.

Olsen, Jens Peter: Frederiksberg Slot, Hærens Officersskole 1997.

Polak, Ada: Gamle vinglass, Oslo 1974.

Rist, v. P. Fr. Pagebreve, København 1898.

Schama, Simon: The Embarrassment of Riches – An interpretation of Dutch Culture in The Golden Age, London 1987.

Suhr, Ingeborg: Mad, København 1939.

The Smithsonian Illustrated Library of Antiques: Porcelain, USA 1979.

Uldall, Kai: Gammel dansk Fajance, København 1961.

Wilson, John Dover: Life in Shakespeare´s England, London 1951.

Wirgin, Jan: Från Kina till Europa, Stockholm 1998.

World Ceramics. London 1977.